More Praise for Love's Garden

"With accessible style and a deep understanding of mindfulness practices, the authors weave a fascinating tapestry of love stories and guided exercises that can help us save, build, and enrich our frequently troubled and most intimate relationships. The result is a beautiful book which told me many things I should have known but didn't."

—Lourdes Arguelles, Ph.D., Marriage and Family Therapist and Professor of Education and Cultural Studies, Claremont Graduate University

Larry and Peggy are true teachers. They are sincere in their practice and forthright in revealing their hearts to others, making themselves both endearing and highly accessible. Their teachings are profound and immediate, blending the dirt and sweat of every day life with deep truths that resonate outside of time. They remind us, through words and actions, how simple and joyful life is.

—Matther Bortolin, author of *The Dharma of Star Wars*

"*Love's Garden* is a very readable and profound manual for cultivating, healing, and deepening a committed relationship with a beloved one. Peggy and Larry offer a new paradigm for relationships characterized by respect, acceptance, and intimacy with one's self and one's partner. The mindfulness practices are designed for couples to develop tools for bridging differences, transforming hardships, and forging understanding and love. They show us that when we preserve peace, joy and harmony in our most intimate relationships, we simultaneously contribute peace, joy and harmony to our families, our communities and the world."

—Karen Hilsberg, Ph.D., Clinical Psychologist

"What a beautiful and fragrant garden this is! Having just remarried after the death of my wife of 35 years, spending time in *Love's Garden* woke me up, brought tears to my eyes, healed my heart and gave me new ways to love again. Thank you, Peggy and Larry, for sharing your wise-love as a gift to nurture love in this troubled world. I am deeply grateful for your work."

—Robertson Work, former United Nations Principal Policy Advisor

"Do not simply read this book, practice it! There are so many treasures here for cultivating compassion and love in all of our relationships."

—Mark Y. A. Davies, Dean, Wimberly School of Religion
and Graduate Theological Center

"*Love's Garden* offers the reader a beautiful reflection of Peggy and Larry's personal journey as well as an easily accessible translation and application of the teachings of Thich Nhat Hanh.

Larry and Peggy clearly enunciate how relationships can be enhanced and deepened through simple practices. The book includes stories from others who describe how these practices enabled them to grow in love through both joy and suffering. This work is a must companion for those who are engaged in a spiritual partnership and supportive for those who want to extend their loving-kindness to all beings."

—Jerry Braza, Ph.D., Professor at Western Oregon University,
Dharma teacher, and author of *Moment by Moment:
The Art and Practice of Mindfulness*

"*Love's Garden* offers such relational rewards for digging into its rich soil that I look forward to offering it to clients. Its useful and clear practices will be helpful not only for romantic couples, but for parents and children as well. Larry and Peggy invite us into their own romance and their relational struggles, generously revealing how specific mindfulness practices can deepen and smooth the furrows of any relationship."

—Harriet Kimble Wrye, Ph.D.,
American Board of Professional Psychology,
Training and Supervising Psychoanalyst

"There is nothing so humbling or so important as learning to be mindful together. We are deeply indebted to Peggy Rowe and Larry Ward for helping us cultivate insight and compassion within our relationships and our communities. Through their wise teachings, the example of their own lives, and the honest stories they share with us, they help us understand what it means to say that happiness (and suffering) are not individual matters."

—Peter Kollock, Ph.D., Professor of Sociology, UCLA

LOVE'S GARDEN

A Guide to Mindful Relationships

PEGGY ROWE WARD AND LARRY WARD

✪

WE WISH TO DEDICATE
LOVE'S GARDEN TO OUR ROOT TEACHER:

The Venerable Thich Nhat Hanh

✪

AND TO OUR PARENTS:

To Roy Lindsey and Viola Paris Ward,
married in 1946 in Chattanooga, Tennessee.
To Bob and Peg Dunn Grimm, married on
July 3, 1948 in Milwaukee, Wisconsin.
We are grateful for the legacy of love
and devotion we have learned from you.
We aspire to grow in love as gracefully
and beautifully as you.

Parallax Press
P.O. Box 7355
Berkeley, California 94707
www.parallax.org

Parallax Press is the publishing division
of Unified Buddhist Church, Inc.

All foreign terms are in Sanskrit unless stated otherwise.
Cover and text design by Jess Morphew.
Cover photograph by Michele Constantini / Getty Images.
Author photograph by Robert Sorrell.

Thich Nhat Hanh's introduction is from a talk given in July 2007
and from other unpublished material.

Rowe-Ward, Peggy.
 Love's garden : a guide to mindful relationships / Peggy Rowe-Ward
and Larry Ward.
   p. cm.
 ISBN 978-1-888375-73-2
 1. Interpersonal relations—Religious aspects—Buddhism. 2.
Love—Religious aspects—Buddhism. 3. Religious life—Buddhism. I.
Ward, Larry. II. Title.
 BQ5400.R68 2008
 294.3'5677—dc22
           2008006937

1 2 3 4 5 / 12 11 10 09 08

CONTENTS ✿

Thich Nhat Hanh

To commit to another person is to embark on a very adventurous journey. You must be very wise and very patient to keep your love alive so it will last for a long time. The first year of a committed relationship can already reveal how difficult it is. When you first commit to someone, you have a beautiful image of them, and you marry that image rather than the person. When you live with each other twenty-four hours a day, you begin to discover the reality of the other person, which doesn't quite correspond with the image you have of him or of her. Sometimes we're disappointed.

In the beginning you're very passionate. But that passion for the other person may last only a short time—maybe six months, a year, or two years. Then, if you're not skillful, if you don't practice, if you're not wise, suffering will be born in you and in the other person. When you see someone else, you might think you'd be happier with them. In Vietnamese we have a saying: "Standing on top of one mountain and gazing at the top of another, you think you'd rather be standing on the other mountain."

When we commit to a partner, either in a marriage ceremony or in a private way, usually it is because we believe we can be and want to be faithful to our partner for the whole of our life. In the Buddhist tradition we have the practice of the Five Mindfulness Trainings, and the third training is to be faithful to the partner you commit to. That is a challenging practice that requires consistent strong practice. Many of us don't have a lot of models of loyalty and faithfulness around us. The U.S. divorce rate is around fifty percent, and for nonmarried but committed partners the rates are similar or higher.

We tend to compare ourselves with others and to wonder if we have enough to offer in a relationship. Many of us feel unworthy. We're thirsty for truth, goodness, compassion, spiritual beauty, and we're sure these things don't exist within us, so we go looking outside. Sometimes we think we've found the ideal partner who embodies all that is good, beautiful, and true. That person may be a romantic partner, a friend, or a spiritual teacher. We see all the good in that person and we fall in love. After a time, we usually discover that we've had a wrong perception of that person and we become disappointed.

Beauty and goodness are always there in each of us. This is the basic teaching of the Buddha. A true teacher, a true spiritual partner, is one who encourages you to look deeply in yourself for the beauty and love you are seeking. The true teacher is someone who helps you discover the teacher in yourself.

According to the Buddha, the birth of a human being is not a beginning but a continuation, and when we're born, all the different kinds of seeds—seeds of goodness, of cruelty, of awakening—are already inside us. Whether the goodness or cruelty in us is revealed depends on what seeds we cultivate, our actions, and our way of life.

At the moment of his awakening at the foot of the Bodhi tree, the Buddha declared, "How strange—all beings possess the capacity to be awakened, to understand, to love, to be free—yet they allow themselves to be carried away on the ocean of suffering." He saw that, day and night, we're seeking what is already there within us. We can call it Buddha nature, awakened nature, the true freedom that is the foundation for all peace and happiness. The capacity to be enlightened isn't something that someone else can offer to you. A teacher can only help you to remove the nonenlightened elements in you so that enlightenment can be revealed. If you have confidence that beauty, goodness, and the true teacher are in you, and if you take refuge in them, you will practice in a way that reveals these qualities more clearly each day.

Each one of us is sovereign over the territory of our own being and the five elements we are made of. These elements are form (body), feelings, perceptions, mental formations, and consciousness. Our practice is to look deeply into these five elements and discover the true nature of our being—the true nature of our suffering, our happiness, our peace, our fearlessness.

But when we've abandoned our territory; we're not responsible rulers. We haven't practiced and, every day, instead of taking care of our territory, we've run away from it and allowed conflicts and disorder to arise. We're afraid to go back to our territory and face the difficulties and suffering. Whenever we have fifteen "free" minutes, an hour or two, we have the habit of using television, newspapers, music, conversation, or the telephone to forget and to run away from the reality of the elements that make up our being. We think, "I'm suffering too much, I have too many problems. I don't want to go back to them anymore."

We have to come back to our physical selves and put things in order. The Buddha gave us very concrete practices which show us how to do this. He was very clear that to clean up and transform the elements of our selves, we need to cultivate the energy of mindfulness. This is what will give us the strength to come back to ourselves.

The energy of mindfulness is something concrete that can be cultivated. When we practice walking mindfully, our solid, peaceful steps cultivate the energy of mindfulness and bring us back to the present moment. When we sit and follow our breathing, aware of our in- and out-breath, we are cultivating the energy of mindfulness. When we have a meal in mindfulness, we invest all our being in the present moment and are aware of our food and of those who are eating with us. We can cultivate the energy of mindfulness while we walk, while we breathe, while we work, while we wash the dishes or wash our clothes. A few days practicing like this can increase the energy of mindfulness in you, and that energy will help you, protect you, and give you courage to go back to yourself, to see and embrace what is there in your territory.

There are real painful feelings, strong emotions, troubling perceptions that agitate or make us afraid. With the energy of mindfulness, we can spend time with these difficult feelings without running away. We can embrace them the way a parent embraces a child and say to them, "Darling, I am here for you; I have come back; I'm going to take care of you." This is what we do with all our emotions, feelings, and perceptions.

When you begin to practice Buddhism, you begin as a part-time Buddha and slowly you become a full-time Buddha. Sometimes you fall back and become a part-time Buddha again, but with steady practice you become a full-time Buddha again. Buddhahood is within reach because, like the Buddha, you're a human being. You can become a Buddha whenever you like; the Buddha is available in the here and now, anytime, anywhere. When you are a part-time Buddha, your romantic relationships may go well some of the time. When you are a full-time Buddha, you can find a way to be present and happy in your relationship full-time, no matter what difficulties arise.

Becoming a Buddha is not so difficult. A Buddha is someone who is enlightened, capable of loving and forgiving. You know that at times you're like that. So enjoy being a Buddha. When you sit, allow the Buddha in you to sit. When you walk, allow the Buddha in you to walk. Enjoy your practice. If you don't become a Buddha, who will?

Every single person contains the seeds of goodness, kindness, and enlightenment. We all have the seed of Buddha nature.

To give the Buddha a chance to manifest in yourself and your loved ones, you have to water those seeds. When we act as if people have these seeds inside them, it gives us and them the strength and energy to help these seeds grow and flower. If we act as if we don't believe in our inherent goodness, we blame others for our suffering and we lose our happiness.

You can use the goodness in yourself to transform your suffering and the tendency to be angry, cruel, and afraid. But you don't want to throw your suffering away because you can use it. Your suffering is compost that gives you the understanding to nourish your happiness and the happiness of your loved one.

TWO GARDENS

You have two gardens: your own garden and that of your beloved. First, you have to take care of your own garden and master the art of gardening. In each one of us there are flowers and there is also garbage. The garbage is the anger, fear, discrimination, and jealousy within us. If you water the garbage, you will strengthen the negative seeds. If you water the flowers of compassion, understanding, and love, you will strengthen the positive seeds. What you grow is up to you.

If you don't know how to practice selective watering in your own garden, then you won't have enough wisdom to help water the flowers in the garden of your beloved. In cultivating your own garden well, you also help to cultivate her garden. Even a week of practice can make a big difference. You are more than intelligent enough to do the work. You need to take your situation in hand and not allow it to get out of control. You can do it. Every time you practice walking mindfully, investing your mind and body in every step, you are taking your situation in hand. Every time you breathe in and know you are breathing in, every time you breathe out and smile to your out-breath, you are yourself, you are your own master, and you are the gardener in your own garden. We are relying on you to take good care of your garden, so that you can help your beloved to take care of hers.

When you have succeeded with yourself and with your beloved, you become a Sangha—a community of two people—and now you can be a refuge for a third person, and then for a fourth, and so on. In this way, the Sangha will grow. There is mutual understanding between you and your beloved. When mutual understanding is there and communication is good, then happiness is possible, and the two of you can become a refuge for others.

If you have a difficult relationship, and you want to make peace with the other person, you have to go home to yourself. You have to go home to your garden and cultivate the flowers of peace, compassion, understanding, and joy. Only after that can you come to your partner and be patient and compassionate.

When we marry or commit to another person, we make a promise to grow together, sharing the fruit and progress of practice. It is our responsibility to take care of each other. Every time the other person does something in the direction of change and growth, we should show our appreciation.

If you have been together with your partner for some years, you may have the impression that you know everything about this person, but it's not so. Scientists can study a speck of dust for years, and they still don't claim to understand everything about it. If a speck of dust is that complex, how can you know everything about another person? Your partner needs your attention and your watering of his or her positive seeds. Without that attention, your relationship will wither.

We have to learn the art of creating happiness. If during your childhood, you saw your parents do things that created happiness in the family, you already know what to do. But many of us didn't have these role models and don't know what to do. The problem is not one of being wrong or right, but one of being more or less skillful. Living together is an art. Even with a lot of goodwill, you can still make the other person very unhappy. The substance of the art of making others happy is mindfulness. When you are mindful, you are more artful.

You and your partner each have a garden to water, but the two gardens are connected. We have two hands and we have names for them, right hand and left hand. Have you ever seen the two hands fighting each other? I have never seen this. Every time my finger gets hurt, I notice that my right hand comes naturally to help my left hand. So there must be something like love in the body. Sometimes they help each other, sometimes they each act separately, but they have never fought.

My right hand invites the bell, writes books, does calligraphy, and pours tea. But my right hand doesn't seem to be proud of it. It doesn't look down on the left hand to say, "Oh left hand, you are good for nothing. All the poems, I wrote them. All the calligraphy in German, French, and English—I've done it all. You are useless. You are good for nothing." The right hand has never suffered from the complex of pride. The left hand has never suffered from the complex of unworthiness. It's wonderful.

When the right hand has a problem, the left hand comes right away. The right hand never says, "You have to pay me back. I always come to help you. You owe me."

When you can see your partner as not separate from you, not better or worse or even equal to you, then you have the wisdom of nondiscrimination. We see the happiness of others as our happiness. Their suffering is our suffering.

Look into your hand. The fingers are like five brothers and sisters from the same family. Suppose we are a family of five. If you remember that if one person suffers, you all suffer, you have the wisdom of nondiscrimination. If the other person is happy, you are also happy. Happiness is not an individual matter.

Our goal in practicing mindfulness and the deepest gift it can bring us is the wisdom of nondiscrimination. We are not noble by birth. We are noble only by virtue of the way we think, speak, and act. The person who practices true love has the wisdom of nondiscrimination and it informs all his actions. He doesn't discriminate between himself and his partner or between his partner and all people. This person's heart has grown large and his love knows no obstacles.

INTRODUCTION

A Garden Map

Each moment from all sides rushes to us the call to love.
We are running to contemplate its vast green field.
Do you want to come with us?

—Rumi

Welcome to *Love's Garden*. We invite you to step in. A garden, like a relationship, is constantly growing and transforming. A garden, like a relationship, requires care, attention, weeding, watering, harvesting, and times of rest.

We have been married for fourteen years, but this is not just a book for married couples. We are Buddhist teachers, but this is not a Buddhist book, though much of what we are sharing is from our sixteen years of practicing as a couple with our teacher, Thich Nhat Hanh. Thich Nhat Hanh married us in 1994 at Plum Village. We would like to offer the practices that have brought more happiness into our home, beauty into our gardens, taught us how to love our compost, and have helped us extend our hearts in the world.

Reading *Love's Garden* is an opportunity for you to acquaint yourself with the techniques of mindfulness practice. Mindfulness is an inherent human capacity for living and being joyful in the present moment. We offer guided meditations, journal exercises, drawing exercises, walks in nature, and rituals that can help in your transformation. Most of the exercises in this book can be done by yourself or with your partner.

The book is an invitation to live life with a larger heart. Because loving one's self is essential before one can love others, Part One explores the art of authentic self-love. We explore true love and offer our experience with the ancient teachings of loving kindness. The mind of love and the seed of awakening are in each of us. Discovering our seeds of awakening and being touched by the mind of love is an invitation to give ourselves a deep chance.

Part One also contains the primary gardening tools of mindful breathing, mindful awareness, and body scanning. Mindfulness is an inherent human capacity for alertness, awareness, and remembering. Meditation is a tool for training our mind to relax, understand, and build its mindfulness muscles. By bringing awareness to our own breath, being, and actions, we begin to treat ourselves gently and allow the seed of love to start to grow. We focus on the four aspects to self-love: observation, acceptance, friendship, and self-cultivation.

Part Two examines how these seeds of love can help blossom into the full beauty of a loving relationship. The core practices of respect, offering, communication, and protection form a nourishing and open place for love to take root and grow. We also address the seeds of suffering that can manifest in relationships and offer practices of healing, forgiveness, and transformation.

Finally, Part Three calls us beyond the boundaries of self and partnership to loving the whole of creation. With mindfulness, we can see there is no difference between loving ourselves, our dear ones, and the whole world. We can bring with us the peace, understanding, and compassion we have gained in our love's journey into the challenging situations and times in which we live.

HOW TO USE THIS BOOK

If you and your partner are looking to deepen the spiritual aspects of your relationship, *Love's Garden* can help you make spirituality and mindfulness a regular part of your life. It can also show you different doors out of difficulties in your relationship.

But while much of this book is focused on a family or a two-person relationship, this book may also be helpful in building your larger spiritual community. We know of some spiritual practice communities, called *sanghas* in Buddhism, which use the practices of love in this book and meet in discussion groups to share their insights and discoveries.

In this book you'll find the word "practice" used quite often. If you've taken music lessons or played a sport, you already have experience with practice. When you practice something, you build skills, discover strengths, and notice where you need to place your attention. The more you practice something correctly, the easier it gets and the more accomplished you become. The practices in this book are simple and easy. The benefit comes from doing them over and over, so that they become a natural part of your life.

PART ONE

Loving Yourself

CHAPTER ONE

The Roots of Love

🍃

Shall we compare our hearts to a garden—with beautiful blooms, strag-gling weeds, swooping birds and sunshine and rain—and most impor-tantly, seeds?

—Greg Livington

Picture the lotus flower. In Buddhist art, the Buddha is often depicted sitting on a lotus flower throne. The lotus represents our own peace and happiness and our innate yearn-ing for the peace and happiness of others. Compassion resides in each of us naturally, but we need to create space in our heart and mind for it to be nurtured and to allow it to flower. Benefit-ing others brings us joy, and our mind and heart become bigger when we care for, think about, and act in the interest of others.

The teachings on true love offered by the Buddha are called the Four Brahmaviharas. *Vihara* means abode or dwelling place and *brahmavihara* means dwelling place of the god Brahma. These teachings are also referred to as the four immeasurables—

2

loving kindness (*maitri*), compassion (*karuna*), joy (*mudita*), and equanimity (*upeksha*). They are referred to as "immeasurables" because if you practice them, the love in your heart will grow so much it cannot be measured.

LOVING KINDNESS

Maitri is the first aspect of true love, the intention and the capacity to offer joy and happiness. Listening and looking deeply help us to develop this capacity so that we can be a good friend to ourselves and to others. Some Buddhist teachers define maitri as "loving kindness" because they believe the word "love" has become tarnished in our popular language. Thich Nhat Hanh uses the phrase "true love," encouraging us to restore love to its true meaning.

COMPASSION

The second aspect of true love is karuna, the intention and capacity to lighten sorrow and relieve and transform suffering. Karuna is generally translated as "compassion." To develop compassion in ourselves, we need to practice mindful breathing, deep listening, and deep looking. Looking deeply and listening carefully, you understand the suffering of the other person. You accept him or her, and naturally your love and compassion flow freely. This is the most beautiful practice and the most powerful method of bringing about transformation and healing. Happiness is made of one substance: compassion, and compassion is made of understanding. If you don't have compassion in your heart, you cannot be happy. Cultivating compassion for others, you create happiness for yourself and for the world.

Someone recently asked us the difference between love and compassion. Love is the practice of nonharming in our thinking, in our speech, and in our actions. Compassion is the practice of helping relieve the suffering of others with our own thoughts, actions, and speech.

SHARED JOY

The third aspect of true love is mudita, or joy. True love always brings joy to the ones we love, as well as to ourselves. In this way we can tell if our love is true or not. Is our love increasing the joy of those we love, or is it stifling them or making them miserable? If the love we offer does not bring joy to both ourself and our beloved, then it's not true love.

Joy is filled with peace and contentment. It is settled, solid, and light at the same time. We delight in the happiness of others. There is no jealousy and we can feel this happiness in our own being.

EQUANIMITY

The fourth element of true love is upeksha, which means equanimity and nonattachment. *Upa* means "over," and *iksh* means "to look." With upeksha, we can see our whole garden. We don't favor one flower over the other or only take care of one patch while leaving the rest to wither and wilt. If our love has clinging, attachment, prejudice, or discrimination, it is not true love.

Upeksha is the wisdom of letting go. Without upeksha, our love can become possessive. If you say you love someone but don't understand his aspirations, needs, and challenges, then your love is a prison. True love allows us to preserve the freedom of our beloved along with our own freedom.

Until we're able to embrace ourselves with love and care, our capacity to offer true love to others remains very limited. One day the Buddha gave a teaching about the earth's capacity to receive, embrace, and transform. He said we should learn to be like the earth, because no matter what people pour on the earth, whether milk, perfume, flowers, jewels, urine, excrement, or mucus, the earth receives them all without discrimination. This is because the earth is immense, so it has the capacity to receive, embrace, and transform. If you cultivate your heart so that it is open, you become immense like the earth and can embrace anyone or anything without suffering.

If you put a handful of salt in a bowl of water and stir it, the water becomes undrinkable. But if you put that salt in a river, it's not affected because the river is so great. If your heart is large like the river, you won't suffer because of small problems. Our practice is to cultivate the four aspects of true love—loving kindness, compassion, joy, and equanimity—that have the capacity to receive, embrace, and transform everything.

WHAT IS LOVE?

Yes, we are loaded with romantic ideas of love. Some are idealized and others are tragic. Our sources for these images come from our family and friends and through cultural conditioning in films, plays, books, poems and, of course, personal experience. Let's take a look at one person's story about love.

In *The Story of My Life* (1996), Helen Keller has a clear memory of the first time that she asked her teacher, Miss Sullivan, for the meaning of the word "love." Miss Sullivan had spelled out the words 'I love you Helen" onto her hand. Helen asked Ms. Sullivan, "what is love?" and she pointed to her heart. She didn't understand. She touched a flower and asked if that was love, or the feeling of the warm sun on her body. Miss Sullivan kept shaking her head. It wasn't the sun, the flower, the warm breeze. She then spelled the word "think" and touched her forehead.

Helen was puzzled. Later in the day there was a shower and then the sun broke through the grey clouds with brilliant light. "Is that not love?" she asked and Miss Sullivan shook her head. She told Helen, "You cannot touch love either; but you feel the sweetness that it pours into everything. Without love you would not be happy or want to play." Helen relates that these words led to her realization about love. "The beautiful truth burst upon my mind—I felt like there were invisible lines stretched between my spirit and the spirits of others."

Love's Garden is about the practice of true love. What is your realization about love and the practice of true love? This exploration may offer some clues to your own unique style of gardening. Or it might be a way to track your journey of discovery while learning from the great teacher that is love.

We offer three different ways to explore: journaling, drawing, or walking. Choose the one that makes you smile.

PRACTICE: *Journaling About Love*

A suggestion is to keep a *Love's Garden* journal. Take out your journal and set aside some quiet time. Sit comfortably for 5–10 minutes. Pay attention to and enjoy each breath. Do you remember the first time you learned about love? Here are some writing prompts:

> *The first time I knew love …*
> *What I learned from my family about love …*
> *Messages I learned about love from my society are …*
> *My feelings about love are …*
> *I remember hearing the word* love *when …*
> *I use the word* love *…*
> *The day I knew love was real …*

PRACTICE: *Drawing Love*

Get out your favorite art supplies—paper, paints, colored pencils, markers, or collage supplies. Have them handy. Sit comfortably and enjoy 5–10 minutes of mindful breathing. Enjoy the rise and fall of each breath. Now say to yourself silently or aloud the word "love" and the words "true love." What are the faces of love? Does love have a color? Does love come in symbols? Does love have a form, shape, song, or smell? Explore some of the images and then end your reflection time and capture your journey with your art supplies.

PRACTICE: *A Walking Meditation on Love*

Take a mindful walk in a place of natural beauty. Walk slowly and silently and enjoy each step. Enjoy the sensation of your feet connecting with the earth. With each step, breathe in the fresh air, and breathe out. Breathe in the sunshine, green boughs of trees, and the sensation of the air on your face. Enjoy every step and every breath.

After about 5–10 minutes, look around and see what draws your attention. It may be a rock, a bird, butterfly, a river, flower, tree, cloud, or a leaf. Choose one object or being from the natural world. Take a few minutes to focus your mind and heart on this object or being. What can you learn about love from this natural teacher? Listen with your inner ear. What lessons of love are being offered in nature?

CHAPTER TWO

Mindfulness Practices

Pay attention. Attention is love.
And love without attention is just a word.
—Karen Maezen Miller

To open the gate of attention is to touch and be touched by the energy of mindfulness. Mindfulness is defined by Thich Nhat Hanh as "the miracle by which we master and restore ourselves." To restore ourselves is to love ourselves.

To enter the gate is a choice to nourish our inherent seed of mindfulness, our capacity for alertness, awareness, and to respect the gift of our precious life. As we cross over this threshold through the practices of conscious breathing, we can witness the miracle of mindfulness. To restore ourselves is to love ourselves.

Some have translated mindfulness as "peacefully remaining" and "calm abiding." To remain with ourselves is a powerful thing. Several wonders are accomplished through this practice.

First, the scattered, fragmented, or warring parts of ourselves are brought together and become harmonious. Secondly, our unsettled emotions, negativity and anger are defused. We learn not to repress, deny or indulge our suffering and unhappiness. We learn the art of becoming friends with our whole selves as we practice embracing ourselves with kindness and generosity.

In addition, this practice helps us to wash off the dust and the grime that have blocked us from being in touch with our essential nature of goodness. Our unkindness dissolves and we no longer contribute to harm. Our true nature—our good heart that radiates loving kindness and goodwill—is revealed. We become truly useful to ourselves and others and available to life.

To help us understand ourselves better, Buddhist psychology describes our consciousness as being composed of eight parts. Here we wish to highlight two of these parts: mind consciousness and store consciousness. Imagine a circle with a horizontal line across the center. The upper part, the part of which we can be aware, is called mind consciousness. The lower part is called store consciousness. Store consciousness is like a garden, a plot of earth that contains all the seeds. Mind consciousness is the gardener.

Our practice is to be the gardener who identifies, waters, and cultivates the best seeds. We need some faith that there are good seeds within us, and then, with appropriate attention, we touch those seeds while we practice sitting meditation and walking meditation and while we go about our daily activities. When we succeed in touching our positive seeds once, we will know how to touch them again and again, and they will strengthen.

As gardeners, we turn the soil, sow seeds, water them, pull weeds, and add fertilizer. But we can't do the work of the earth. Only the earth can hold the seeds and bring forth the fruits of our labor. What's most important is that the gardener has faith in the earth and entrusts to it seeds he considers to be important. Store consciousness has the power to maintain, nourish, and bring forth.

The practice of meditation has two parts: *samatha*, stopping; and *vipashyana*, deep looking. Samatha means we slow down our thinking and relax and calm our body and mind. Vipashyana means we look deeply to have insight into the true nature of things, including our suffering and its causes. In the practice of meditation, we trust our store consciousness. We nourish a seed in the soil of our store consciousness, we water and care for that seed, and we trust that one day the seed will sprout and bring forth plants, flowers, and fruits.

The gardener knows that it is the earth that brings forth the sprouting of the seeds and that his job is simply to take care of the earth. Through the practice of mindfulness, mind consciousness nourishes the positive seeds in store consciousness. This is done day and night, like a gardener working nonstop. In this way, mind consciousness helps store consciousness bring forth the fruits of joy, peace, and transformation.

When mindfulness touches beautiful, positive seeds, it helps these seeds develop and reveal themselves more clearly. When it touches negative seeds, it helps those seeds to transform. The gardener must practice mindfulness in order to recognize and identify the positive seeds in store consciousness and help them grow.

> *To treasure the breath is like loving your face and your eyes. It has never been unattainable.*
> —Master Great Nothing of Sung-Shen

MINDFUL BREATHING

Thich Nhat Hanh begins his talks by inviting us to meditate with the sound of the bell, and to enjoy our breathing. Breathing is the most important tool we have to change our consciousness. This is good news, because breathing is one of the simplest things in the world. It costs nothing and you never have to worry about forgetting it at home or locking it in the car. The practice of mindful breathing is simply to be aware that you are breathing. To keep your awareness with your breath, you can say silently, "Breathing in, I know I'm breathing in. Breathing out, I know I'm breathing out." Or if you prefer, you can just say, "in" as you breathe in and "out" as you breathe out. As we continue to follow our breathing, we notice it grows deeper and slower and tension leaves our body. We should never force the breath; the breath becomes more relaxed quite naturally as we maintain our awareness of it.

The challenge is not in the breathing, which is automatic, but in the noticing. To reclaim that which has always been a part of your experience requires your active awareness, alertness, and participation.

Watching the breath can help you slow down, relax, and bring body and mind together. Noticing the breath helps you tune in to yourself and your body and come back to the present moment. We have the tendency to get lost in our thoughts, regrets about the past, worries about the future, or strong emotions in the present—our body is here but our mind is somewhere else. Conscious breathing brings our mind back to our body again.

Breathing is our fundamental connection to life itself and is inseparable from our health. Breathing affects not only our respiratory system, but also our neurological, cardiovascular, gastrointestinal, and muscular systems—our whole body and mind. Breathing affects our energy, sleep, memory, and ability to concentrate. Breathing influences our every action.

GUIDELINES FOR SITTING MEDITATION

- The spine is upright with its natural curve. Imagine the spine like a stack of golden coins. There will be a soft curve.
- Rest your hands gently and comfortably on your thighs.
- Relax your arms and shoulders.
- Relax the back of the neck. This helps your chin to drop a little. It puts tension in your body to have your chin jutting out or stuck in like a turtle.
- You can experiment with having your eyes closed or having the eyelids half shut with your gaze softened and directed toward the floor.
- Your jaw, face, forehead are soft, natural and relaxed.

+ If you are on a cushion, keep your ankles loosely crossed. If you are on a chair, have both feet firmly on the floor.

MINDFUL BREATHING

Mindful breathing helps us to train our minds to observe ourselves without blame or judgment. To begin, take a deep breath and completely relax. Settle into your self, calming and uniting body and mind. Wait for the breath to arise naturally. Without effort or sound, breathe in and breathe out. Notice everything just as it is, without any desire to change it. Watch the breath with an open, nonjudgmental awareness. Be present, aware, wakeful, and relaxed.

+ Be aware of your breathing. The breath will present itself. Notice your breathing without trying to change or alter it in any way. Just let your breath be.
+ Rest your attention on your inhalation for the entire length of the inhalation.
+ Rest your attention on your exhalation. Again, notice the entire length of the exhalation.
+ Do this five times, enjoying the sensation of the breath entering and leaving your body.
· Repeat this practice several times through your day. You may wish to post a note to remind yourself of your breathing practice. Experiment at different times and in different settings.

> *Meditation is like digging deep into the ground until we reach the purest water. We look deeply into ourselves until insight arises and our love flows to the surface. Practicing love and happiness, joy radiates from our eyes and everyone around us benefits from our smile and our presence.*
>
> —Thich Nhat Hanh

MINDFUL WALKING

Another enjoyable way to practice awareness of the breath is mindful walking. This is a very simple practice. The purpose of mindful walking is to help our body and mind to be in the same place—to be right here, right now. Where life is happening. We have this tendency to rush or to be focused on the next place where we are going. This is a very simple practice. We are walking just to be walking. We are not trying to arrive anyplace or go anywhere. We walk to walk.

Whenever we walk, whether it's from the car to the office or from the kitchen to the living room, we can walk in peace and joy, arriving in each step. Our awareness is with our breath and steps; we synchronize our steps with our breath, taking two or three steps for each in-breath and two or three steps for each out-breath. It may help to slow down our normal walking pace a little. If we take three steps for each in-breath and each out-breath, we can say, "In, in, in. Out, out, out."

Peggy has some specific practices that help her to be solid and available to life. She uses conscious breathing as she arrives home after a day of work. This helps her to make the transition from work to home. She also uses walking meditation on the cancer ward where she works as a chaplain. She made it a dedicated practice, and now her body remembers when sometimes her mind will forget.

PRACTICE: *Walking Meditation*

Set aside 10 minutes for silent mindful walking. Begin by connecting with your breath and follow your breath. Then connect with your feet and the sensation of your feet on the ground. Begin slow walking and you can say the words "In" with the in-breath and "Out" with the out-breath. Find your rhythm which will be approximately 2–3 steps for each breath. Feel the sensation of your foot as the ball of the foot and the heel connect with the earth. Enjoy. You are doing the practice correctly if you are enjoying your walking.

Morning Walk

KIM HSIEH

A cool grey fog hangs delicately in the air. Moisture gathers in tiny silvery beads on my black jacket. I take in the feel of my stride along the pavement, the gentle damp breeze, my reflection flitting by on the windows and storefronts.

A woman stands in front of her store, spraying down the sidewalk with a hose. The look in her eyes is faintly absent as she directs the water from side to side and then toward the street, a fine mist of spray bounding up and getting caught in her thinning hair. As I approach the periphery of the wet sidewalk, she snaps off the water and does not look up. As I am about to pass, she glances at me and our eyes meet for a moment. My contentment spills over and I smile at her. There is a brief hesitation and then she smiles back. The warmth of her response surprises me, fills me. The warmth of that fleeting smile lingers in me and stays with me as I descend into the train station.

"Oops." I shrug my shoulders and half-smile at the woman I pass on the stairs as I watch my train pull away from the platform. She smiles back, maybe in sympathy, and I feel as if we've just shared a quiet little joke. In a few minutes, another train pulls up and I step in. The door closes, then opens again. In the pregnant pause before the doors close once more, a woman and her young son burst triumphantly through the doors breathless and giggling and take a seat near me. Their sense of fun is contagious and I laugh with them, smiling at the woman. She smiles back, acknowledging me, and then says something in Spanish to her son as they settle into their seats.

I get off at Grant Avenue. Ahead of me, a youngish man in a striped shirt is shoveling sand into a pail from a pile at the side of the road. He moves with a steady, relaxed rhythm, finishes his task, turns to move the pail. As I pass, he looks up and I smile at him. He flashes a broad smile in response, the warmth of his brown eyes lighting his entire face. It's almost too much and I look away, then wish I hadn't. The moment is gone and I continue down the hill, a light mixture of regret, satisfaction and pleasure lingering in the air behind me.

When giving instructions for meditation, my teacher often suggests relaxing facial muscles by allowing a half-smile to come to your face. "It is the same smile you see on the face of the Buddha," he says. When I first heard this instruction years ago, it seemed artificial, like "putting on a happy face." I didn't yet have a deep understanding of his words. But this morning in San Francisco, I sense the transformative power of such a small act and its ability to open one's heart to the possibility of true connection, of love and understanding, in every moment, with every being.

THERE IS A BODY HERE

We experience our life through our body. To love ourselves fully is to become intimate with ourselves. Self love first of all requires the courage to come home to ourselves in the here and now and to recognize that there is a body here. Mindful breathing helps us to train our minds to observe ourselves and others without blame or judgment.

When we are mindful of our breath and our body, the body becomes the object of mindfulness. This means that the body becomes mindfulness. Love needs an object. When we breathe in and embrace our body, our body is our mindfulness and our mindfulness is our body. There is no distinction between subject and object.

When we bring our attention to our body and embrace our body with our mindfulness we experience love. By looking deeply into our body, we can discover many things—such as a sore knee, or the feeling of tiredness, loneliness, fear or happiness. We may discover that our body loved taking a walk or that we need to take better care of our body. This can be why our body will experience harmony or disharmony, stability or happiness. We practice love for our body by bringing our loving attention to our body, holding it mindfully and tenderly. This helps our body to become calm.

We have benefited from body scanning practices for many years. We do them before getting out of bed each morning. We take our first 5–10 minutes to breathe into our body to enter the day solid and alive. Better yet, we can truly say, "there is a body here."

PRACTICE: *Body Scanning*

Please find a quiet place where you will not be disturbed. Have a pen or drawing supplies and your journal or paper nearby. Lie down in a comfortable position on your bed, couch, blanket or yoga mat where you can stretch out with ease and feel balanced.

Gently close your eyes. Place your mindfulness on the rising and falling of your abdomen. Stay with this experience of the breath for a few minutes, until the breath naturally becomes calmer and slower.

Imagine your mindfulness energy as a beam of light. Scan your body beginning with the bottom of your feet. You are scanning your body with the energy of light and the energy of mindfulness. You are not looking for anything special, you are just noticing.

Bring the light of your attention from side to side moving slowly across the body. Scan both feet with the light of mindfulness and slowly move up the body until you reach the top of your head. Once you are at the crown, pause for a moment and enjoy several breaths.

Move your mindfulness beam from your crown down your body. Set your intention to bring the energy and quality of loving kindness to your brain, eyes, ears, jaw, mouth, neck, throat, heart. Pause for a few moments at your heart and send your radiant light of loving kindness to your heart. Then continue to scan down through the lungs, abdomen, liver, kidneys, spleen, stomach and pelvic region.

Continue to move your beam of light down the body, mindfully breathing with your thighs, legs, knees, ankles, and feet. Let your beam of mindfulness return to where you began at your feet. Now feel yourself breathing through the soles of your feet all the way to the top of your head. Take a moment to rest in this stillness and peace. When you are complete, turn on either side and gently come to a sitting position.

Take a moment to ask yourself what you noticed. How is your body in this moment? What did you see, feel, hear, observe? Where is your body feeling well and hearty? Were any places missing from your awareness? Were you aware of any pain or suffering? This aspect of meditation is called deep looking. It can be helpful to journal your notes on the practice of the body scan, or to make a quick sketch of your body.

CHAPTER THREE

Coming Home to Self

The imagery of inviting all parts of ourselves home, back to the table, like the prodigal son, lies at the heart of the Aramaic sense of what it means to be perfect.

—Neil Douglas-Klotz, *The Hidden Gospel*

A TRUE FRIENDSHIP

The best thing you can do for your relationship is to begin to learn to fully love yourself. This self-love will not make you more inward or selfish. Rather it is only the person who truly loves him- or herself who is able to offer that love outward. There is a Buddhist sutra called the Raja (King). In this teaching story, the Buddha states that no being is more precious to us than our own self. King Pasenadi of Koshala asks his queen, Mallika, who is the one in the world who is the most dear to her. He expects her answer to be that it is he, her husband. But she answers that it is she herself who is most dear to her. The king realizes that the same is true for him, that no one is as dear to him as he is himself. The king and queen go to ask the Buddha about this, and he confirms their discovery with this teaching:

> *I visited all quarters with my mind*
> *nor found I any dearer than myself;*
> *self is likewise to every other dear;*
> *who loves himself may never harm another.*

According to the Buddha, every creature holds itself most dear of all; every being wants to live and thrive. Our recognition of this is the basis of our compassion for ourselves and others: "who loves himself may never harm another." Through the practice of loving and understanding you will feel your heart grow to include more people and beings. We practice "selective watering," watering the most beautiful seeds in ourselves and in our beloved.

A good friend accepts you just as you are. You can tell when someone wants to change you; it doesn't feel good. The same is true when we critique ourselves. To be able to love your partner and others in the world, you need to first practice being that good friend to yourself and accepting yourself completely. This requires looking deeply at ourselves without flinching and accepting the whole of what we discover. If we say, "I'll love you when you lose ten pounds," or "You must do this or that before I can love you," then we aren't being a true friend.

Once we realize we're the closest and most precious person on Earth to ourselves, we'll stop treating ourselves as an enemy.

The conditions for happiness are present and available to us right now, without us having to improve ourselves. As we grow in acceptance of ourselves, we become a safer, kinder, gentler place to inhabit for ourselves and for others.

Several years ago, we had the good fortune of joining Thich Nhat Hanh, monks, nuns, and other laypeople on a tour of China. An elderly monk with a wide grin and gentle gait was our tour guide at a monastery in the south. We stepped into a large meditation room. The only object in the room was a large oval mirror placed in the center of the room. The monk turned to us with an engaging grin, pointed to the mirror and said, "Advanced practice."

METTA PRACTICE

How do you talk to yourself? Whose voice is it? Is the voice critical or loving? Are you in touch with a sacred voice that you hear within? This constant inner conversation is the basis of the love relationship that we have with ourselves.

Metta is a practice of uncovering the brilliance of light and love that rests in each of us. This radiance is often covered up with ignorance, fear, anger, and the wounds from life experience, but it is there. Metta comes from the Sanskrit word *mitra*, which means friend. We begin by befriending ourselves, learning to talk kindly and sweetly to ourselves, learning to offer ourselves a blessing instead of a curse or a complaint. Actively being a loving friend to your own self is the foundation of the practice.

The practice is simple. We gently repeat phrases that are

meaningful in terms of what we wish for ourselves and, eventually, for others.

We begin by offering metta to ourselves. There are four phrases used in classic Buddhist teachings:

> *May I be free from danger.*
> *May I have mental happiness.*
> *May I have physical happiness.*
> *May I have ease of well-being.*

May I be free from danger. With this prayer, we are touching the wish that all beings have for protection, safety, and a place of refuge. We have the aspiration that all beings may be free from accidents, external strife, and external violence. Our heart's desire is that everyone can have a place of safe haven. Other phrases for this meditation might include "May I be safe and free from injury," "May I have safety," or "May I have a safe place."

May I have mental happiness. Even in the best of circumstances, we can make ourselves suffer with our own mind. Mental happiness is a mind that is free from anger, affliction, fear, and anxiety. Mental happiness arises through looking at ourselves with the eyes of understanding and love. Then we practice by recognizing and touching the seeds of joy and happiness in ourselves. We also learn to identify and see the sources of anger, craving, and delusion in ourselves. Other phrases people sometimes use are "May I be happy," "May I be peaceful," or "May I be liberated."

May I have physical happiness. With this we are wishing ourselves a healthy and happy body. We touch the deep aspiration that all beings experience a life without physical pain. We're in touch with our desire that no one experience ill health and physical suffering. Other phrases might be "May I be healthy," "May I embody vibrant health," or "May I be healed."

May I have ease of well-being. With this phrase, we are addressing our everyday life. We are touching the wish that our lives be filled with the energies of grace and harmony rather than struggle and conflict. We aspire to live in a way that we experience solidity, freshness, and freedom. We pray for well-being, peace, and lightness and to be spared from strife. Other phrases could be "May I dwell in peace," "May I experience ease," or "May I live in harmony."

LOVING KINDNESS

When we practice being a good friend to ourselves, we are practicing the art of loving kindness. Loving kindness can be described as our ability to bring joy to ourselves and others. The basis of loving kindness is understanding and acceptance. We practice it first with ourselves, looking deeply at our own self and accepting what we find. With practice, love will arise more and more often. We will feel a natural desire to go in the direction of what is good, true, and beautiful.

You may feel rusty about how to treat yourself with loving kindness. To begin, it may be helpful for you to recall a time when you were moved by the loving kindness of another person. When we reflect on goodness, we think of small acts of kindness, like saying good morning, offering a cup of tea, giving a welcoming smile, a warm hug, or scratching Larry's dog Reggae's ears. Here is Peggy's memory of goodness:

> I remember driving home several days after my husband, Steve's passing. As I stepped out of my car, I noticed something colorful on the front porch. Walking up the steps, I realized that it was a pile of toys and games. There were a number of dolls, a fire truck, and a board game. I picked up a small, bright-blue plush toy that had black and white eyes, it made me smile, something that I hadn't done in days. That evening, I received calls from two of my friends. They told me that when their children learned of Steve's death, they insisted that they be driven to my house where they left their favorite toys and games. The mothers insisted that it was the idea of the children.

Larry remembers his first golf lesson with Peggy's mother:

> My feet are slipping on the practice green, slipping in my nongolf shoes. I notice the sign in this backcountry golf course that says "No Cowboy Boots. No High Heels" and I know I am far from the 'hood. I recall my father's stories of not being allowed to play golf due to policies of racial discrimination. Something in me quickens as I realize that I am here for my father, too. I am also frustrated. How could something that looks so easy be

so challenging? Peggy's mother says "Oh, Larry, what a lovely day. I'm so happy to be here," and I am awakened to the presence of beauty, the soft breeze from the Idaho mountains, and the gift of friendship. "Here let me help you," she says as she stretches her short arms around my belly. I can feel her heart beat next to mine. She positions the club in my hands. What am I doing on a golf course in Idaho? I am with my friend, and I soften into this offering of love. We practiced for hours, and all I remember is her kindness and gentle coaching.

PRACTICE: *Remembering the Good Within*

Have your journal handy. Settle into a place where you will not be interrupted. Take a few deep breaths and come home to yourself. Enjoy mindful breathing for 5–10 minutes.

Say to yourself the word "goodness." What comes to mind? What colors, images, words or symbols? Recall a recent experience that you might call "goodness." You might start small, remembering an act of goodness you received—a smile, a wave, a welcome, a cup of tea. How about some acts of goodness that you offered. Stay curious and open. Repeat the word "goodness." What do you notice? Is there a sound, vibration, energy, light or sensation that is "goodness"? How would you describe goodness?

Reflect back on your life to a time that you were touched by goodness. When you experienced something that would be "goodness." Call to mind things that you might have said or done that you feel were acts of goodness—a time you were generous, or expressed thoughtfulness, or caring, or contributed to someone's well being. If something comes to mind, breathe into the energy of happiness that might accompany the memory. If nothing comes to mind, reflect on the aspiration for goodness and happiness that resides within you.

Breathing in and out, continue to reflect on the energy and experience of goodness. Goodness given, goodness received, tasted, touched, known. Recall these moments and re-experience the sensation of goodness.

Come back gently and write in your journal or craft, color, or draw what you experienced in remembering goodness.

The practice of true love encourages us to live our life directed by the energy of goodness. At first it helps to be more intentional and to make this a conscious process. We might wake up and actively welcome the day by stating our intention to move in the direction of love, goodness, and happiness. We then can use our own experiences of the day as a teaching device. What does goodness feel like, smell like, tastes like, and sound like? What embodies goodness? What are the faces of goodness? Can I sense it in me and around me?

Practicing in this way, goodness develops into a feedback system, a sensor. It is a kind of homing device that supports us in moving in the direction of goodness. We will have more and more experiences when we feel transported by the energy of goodness itself. We will not need to think. We will feel moved, called, propelled by that which is good, true, and beautiful.

This will happen all on it's own. We know that you have had this experience.

PRACTICE: *Being a Pencil in the Hand of God*

> *I am a little pencil in the hand of a writing God*
> *who is sending a love letter to the world.*
> —Mother Teresa

Select a quiet place for reflection. Have your journal and/or art supplies handy. Enjoy five to ten minutes of mindful breathing.

Recall a time when you experienced "being a pencil in the hand of God." Say to yourself the quote from Mother Teresa, and see if you can recall a time when you felt moved to the energy of love, directed by goodness, held by goodness. What do you notice when you are energetically pulled into love? What do you feel, sense, notice?

When you have completed your meditation, take out your writing or drawing supplies and sketch or write about this experience. If you are writing, use the present tense. This will help make the experience very fresh and current. Say to yourself "I am," "I feel," "I notice," "I see," and so on. Collect these experiences and memories.

LOVING KINDNESS MEDITATION

How do you love and talk to yourself? The inner conversation we conduct at all hours is the basis of the love relationship that we have with ourselves. Whose voice is it that loves or chides you? Is the voice critical or loving? Is there a sacred voice that you hear within?

Loving kindness meditation practice is designed to uncover the brilliance of light and love that dwells in each of us. This radiance is just covered up with ignorance, fear, anger, and the red dust of life. But it is there. We begin by befriending our self, learning to talk kindly and sweetly, learning to offer ourselves a blessing instead of a curse or a complaint. This is the foundation of the practice of true love, actively being a loving friend to our self.

The practice is simple. We kindly and gently repeat the phrases that are referred to as the Heavenly Abodes in classic Buddhist teachings. The phrases are:

> *May I be free from danger*
> *May I have mental happiness*
> *May I have physical happiness*
> *May I have ease of well-being.*

The practice of loving kindness meditation begins by extending these aspirations to our own self. We send these thoughts as a blessing and a prayer. We connect with our aspiration and our heartfelt desire that we experience safety, happiness, good health, and well-being. We connect with these sentiments as energy of light and of love.

31

Chocolate Pudding

ANNA ZILBOORG

I was recently invited to remember the energy of "goodness" and I thought of Raymond. One day, when I was working in the kitchen, Raymond and his four older siblings came barreling into the room. They knew there was leftover popcorn. I handed a bowl of popcorn to one of the taller children, and they all scurried out of the kitchen amid peals of laughter.

I heard a small voice say, "I know where they are going." I looked down and there was Raymond.

"Where are they going, Raymond?" I asked.

"They're hiding from me," he said. He sat on the kitchen floor and played with a small truck. He played quietly and didn't appear to be disturbed.

A short while later, the children all tumbled into the kitchen and laughingly handed Raymond the empty bowl. "Here's your share, Raymond," one of them said. Raymond was right. They had been hiding from him and playing a trick on him.

I remembered there was some leftover pudding from dinner, so I went into the refrigerator and brought out a bowl of chocolate pudding. "Here, Raymond," I said. "There's some chocolate pudding left over from dinner. The children all gathered around him saying how icky pudding is, taunting that no one likes pudding, it looks like poop. Raymond reached out his hands for the bowl of pudding and a smile stretched across his face. "I just love chocolate pudding", he said. He sat down at the table, and all the children gathered around him teasing and prodding and poking at him about nasty pudding. He just kept on spooning it in his mouth and saying, "Mmmm, I just love chocolate pudding." And he smiled through every bite.

In reflecting on the story of Raymond, I think of the sweet, simple goodness of chocolate pudding. I think of a child that didn't fall into negativity. I think of focusing on the present moment, tasting goodness, and not falling into lack or negativity.

PRACTICE: *Loving Kindness Meditation*

1. Find a comfortable, quiet place. You can write down the Heavenly Abodes, the loving kindness phrases and refer to them in your meditation. Take a few breaths and settle in. Mindfully follow your breath and enjoy your breathing. *(5–10 minutes)*

2. Say the word "goodness" to yourself and recall some of your personal memories and recollections of goodness. Reflect on the goodness that is within you and your own aspiration for love and happiness. *(2–5 minutes)*

3. Read or recall the first blessing: "May I be free from danger." Gently repeat the phrase and rest with the feelings and sensations of this self-blessing. See this prayer as a radiant light, the energy of love that you are sending to yourself. If your attention wanders, kindly bring your attention back to your breath and the blessing. *(2–5 minutes)*

4. Read or recall the next blessing: "May I have mental happiness." Repeat the phrase and rest with the energy of this prayer. Allow any feelings or sensations to arise and gently repeat the blessing. *(2–5 minutes)*

5. Read or recall the blessing: "May I have physical happiness." Settle into the feelings that arise and fall with this prayer. Send this energy of light and love

to your physical body. Gently repeat the phrase and rest in the energy of the blessing. *(2–5 minutes)*

6. Read or recall the blessing: "May I have ease of well-being." Settle into the experience of harmony, peace, and ease that are connected to this self blessing. Receive this blessing as an energy of love and touch into your deep desire to have harmony and peace in your life. *(2–5 minutes)*

7. Complete your meditation time by extending the merit of the practice to all beings. Feel free to experiment with the phrases. Be creative. Find the words, images, metaphors, and memories that bring the greatest charge of joy, light, love and ease into your life.

PRACTICE: *You Are Accepted*

Paul Tillich gave a famous sermon with this title—"You Are Accepted." His words are a powerful reminder that we are loved beyond our wildest imagining. True love is first of all to accept ourselves as we actually are. Then what we do for ourselves—any act of acceptance, tolerance, kindness, gentleness, any gift of peace—will affect how we experience the world. This will not happen later. It will happen right now. As we grow in acceptance of ourselves, we become a safer, kinder, gentler place to inhabit for ourselves and for others. We experience peace in coming home to ourself and that peace radiates out into our world, offering unconditional friendship.

+ Settle into a quiet and comfortable place. Enjoy several minutes of mindful breathing. Settle into being in your body.

+ Remind yourself of "goodness" by recalling strong images of goodness and loving kindness. Say the word "goodness" silently or out loud and breathe in goodness. Bring to mind people that have been teachers, role models and mentors. Remember them in your body and imagine them smiling at you in this moment.

+ Say to yourself silently or aloud "I am accepted." Yes, you are accepted by the mystery of life and held in love in this very moment. The grace of this insight allows the flower of compassion for ourselves to bloom.

+ Repeat to yourself silently or out loud "I accept myself just as I am." We find it useful to use our whole name with this practice. Sometimes I use my arms to embrace myself as I repeat the words "I am accepted." Thoughts may arise as well as images. Return to the breath and the phrase "I accept myself".

+ It is helpful to journal about your experience to note how you are growing in acceptance and also where you are experiencing challenges in cultivating compassion for yourself.

+ How will you go about accepting yourself today?

When Sidney Poitier accepted the Lifetime Achievement Award from the American Film Institute, he spoke these words as part of his acceptance speech: "May I be true to myself and useful to the journey." We wrote these words down and have been meditating on them ever since. What does it mean to you to be "true to yourself and useful to the journey"?

CHAPTER FOUR

Self-Cultivation

❧

Live your daily life in a way that you never lose yourself. When you are carried away with your worries, fears, cravings, anger, and desire, you run away from yourself and you lose yourself. The practice is always to go back to oneself.

—Thich Nhat Hanh

By engaging in the practices of observation, acceptance, and offering friendship to ourselves, we are rediscovering and watering the seeds of love in ourselves. This practice begins the internal art of self-cultivation. It takes time, practice, and patience.

To continue on the path of self-cultivation and acceptance, the Buddha offered the Five Precepts. Thich Nhat Hanh has updated them as the Five Mindfulness Trainings. We have indeed found them to be powerfully helpful guidelines for our lives. We understand that these are practices that provide a continuous learning experience for our growth and development as individuals and as a couple.

The Five Mindfulness Trainings

(adapted from *For a Future to Be Possible*, Thich Nhat Hanh, Parallax Press, 2007)

THE FIRST MINDFULNESS TRAINING: REVERENCE FOR LIFE

Aware of the suffering caused by the destruction of life, I am committed to cultivating compassion and learning ways to protect the lives of people, animals, plants, and minerals.

THE SECOND MINDFULNESS TRAINING: GENEROSITY

Aware of the suffering caused by exploitation, social injustice, stealing, and oppression, I am committed to cultivating loving kindness and learning ways to work for the well-being of people, animals, plants, and minerals.

THE THIRD MINDFULNESS TRAINING: SEXUAL RESPONSIBILITY

Aware of the suffering caused by sexual misconduct, I am committed to cultivating responsibility and learning ways to protect the safety and integrity of individuals, couples, families, and society.

THE FOURTH MINDFULNESS TRAINING: DEEP LISTENING AND LOVING SPEECH

Aware of the suffering caused by unmindful speech and the inability to listen to others, I am committed to cultivating loving speech and deep listening in order to bring joy and happiness to others and relieve others of their suffering.

THE FIFTH MINDFULNESS TRAINING: MINDFUL CONSUMPTION

Aware of the suffering caused by unmindful consumption, I am committed to cultivating good health, both physical and mental, for myself, my family, and my society by practicing mindful eating, drinking, and consuming.

Perhaps you are thinking that it would be impossible to live up to these ideals. Please understand The Five Trainings as ways of developing hearts and minds that can embody love and compassion in daily life. We intend them, study them, and practice them as best we can and then we learn about ourselves throughout the process of repetition of the intention, study, and practice. The trainings function as our North Star, as a direction or path for our growth and development of love and compassion. They are an expression of the awakened mind that is directed toward ourselves and others.

This training in higher mind is rooted in the dynamic nature of our interior life. The life of the mind is described in many of the Buddha's insights as a wonder to behold and sometimes as a beast to tame. The practices of meditation are central to realizing this innate potential of higher mind, the foundation of which is samatha, the technique of relaxing and calming our body and mind leading to a state of tranquility.

Samatha practices can result in a mind that is serene, free of confusion, sharp, quick, skillful and happy. Upon the foundation of this tranquility we can learn to improve our attention skills as we enquire into how our minds work and examine our own journey of healing and transforming into love. Through meditation, we can stabilize and refine our best mental capacities and direct ourselves away from the prison of a small sense of self. Our minds begin to naturally open like a flower to its depth of wisdom.

With the practice of vipashyana, or concentration, we train our minds in the techniques of contemplation or deep looking. Through this approach we can gain a mind that can understand what is happening. We come to have knowledge of our suffering, the causes of our suffering, and a way out of suffering. Through this our mind continues its journey in letting go of its over identification with internal and external signs of self and other.

Self-cultivation is training our minds so that we can become capable of wisdom, resulting in our thinking and views going in the direction of openness, goodness and compassion. As we learn to recognize our true self, we can recognize the true nature of reality and its manifestations. Whether this manifestation is an ant or a tree, the wind or the moonlight, Aunt Gladys or your beloved partner, we learn to see life as it is.

The self-cultivated mind becomes free from the addiction of falling in love with the falling in love experience. This mind is able to understand that the experience of romantic love is a real but limited encounter with the energy of self-transcendence. But this mind knows that this is a profoundly impermanent experience and therefore remains free to learn the art of true love.

As we learn to look gently and honestly at ourselves, at our thoughts, feelings, emotions, the great stuff and the less than great stuff, we can see that we have built up a lot of barriers to loving others and ourselves. We may find that we are plum full of rules, opinions, fears, biases, and perceptions we have used to create a false sense of security.

We practice by eliminating these hindrances that dirty our mirror. This means that we work to reconcile the past hurts that have kept us from being clear. This eliminates the endemic sluggishness, exhaustion and insomnia that some of us may feel. The path of self-cultivation helps us to rest more easily so that we have more energy for ourselves, others and the world.

RIGHT EFFORT

Many of us have the intention of watering the positive seeds but find that actually putting this into practice in our lives is very difficult. It's not that we don't want to live more mindfully; rather it's that as we look deeply at ourselves, we can see that we've built up many barriers to loving others and ourselves. We may find that we're full of rules, opinions, fears, biases, and perceptions that we've used to create a false sense of security.

Thich Nhat Hanh reminds us of key practices for clearing through the weeds and watering the seeds of love within us. The Buddha called these practices "Right Effort." The word "right" here does not mean making a judgment or discriminating between right and wrong. Rather, in Buddhism, "right" means cultivating clarity of mind and going in the direction of what is wholesome.

The Four Practices of Right Effort

(adapted from *The Heart of the Buddha's Teaching*,
Thich Nhat Hanh, Parallax Press, 1998)

1. Prevent unwholesome seeds in our store consciousness that have not yet arisen from arising. Choose not to water the negative seeds of doubt, jealousy, and anger. Choose an environment that supports this effort.

2. Help the unwholesome seeds that have already arisen to return to store consciousness. If it happens that a negative seed of doubt, anger, or envy manifests in your mind, ask the seed to go back down. You can do this while walking mindfully, during body scanning, or in sitting meditation.

3. Find ways to water the wholesome seeds in our store consciousness. When a good seed has not had a chance to manifest, take action to help the good seed to manifest. This will help to keep unwholesome seeds from arising and will make the landscape of the mind beautiful by doing something you love, doing something kind for someone else, recalling someone you love, or remembering a happy event.

4. Nourish the wholesome seeds that have already arisen so that they will stay present in our mind consciousness and grow stronger. When a good seed has manifested, try to keep it blooming for a long time. This is like keeping a beloved friend in your garden.

> *Dear God. I'm doing the best that I can. Love, Frank*
> —from *Children's Letters to God*

PRACTICE: *Reconciliation with Oneself*

Set aside some quiet time for mindful breathing and reflection.
Have your journal and/or art supplies handy. Enjoy 5–10 minutes of mindful breathing and coming home to yourself. Then,
as in a guided meditation, invite yourself to look into your heart
and mind and ask the following questions. Between each question, allow some time for your body and mind to communicate.

After sitting with these questions for about 10–15 minutes,
take some time to write or draw your discoveries. We like to
meditate, read the questions, meditate some more, draw a picture of our garden and then write some responses. We find that
both drawings and specific descriptions help us to come home
to ourself.

+ Looking deeply to see: the wholesome mental qualities that are now manifesting in my speech and
  action. Some examples are my patience, creativity,
  kindness, and diligence. How can I help them to
  continue to manifest? How am I currently nourishing these wholesome seeds? How can I celebrate the
  good practice I am doing?
+ Looking deeply to see: the wholesome mental qualities that are not yet manifesting. Some examples

might be my joy of singing if I haven't been singing, my tolerance, and my wisdom mind. Are they below ground or just coming to the surface of the soil? What kind of fertilizer will help them grow?

+ Looking deeply to see: the unwholesome mental qualities that are not yet manifesting in my speech and actions. Some examples of unwholesome mental formations are forgetfulness, fear, greed, confusion, frustration and so on. How am I practicing to keep them in the storehouse of my consciousness? How can I be aware of them before they manifest?

+ Looking deeply to see: the unwholesome mental qualities that are currently manifesting in my speech and actions. What unwholesome mental formations are currently growing in my garden? How are these being nourished? How are these being fed? How can I cut off the food supply so that the blooms can wither and return to being seeds in my storehouse?

Practicing with a Partner

SUSAN GLOGOVAC

Soon after I received the Five Mindfulness Trainings, I found a meditation group. I went to the group every week without my life partner. He always wished me well, and I knew that he was sincere. Still, I felt sad that he was not joining me. I was jealous of those in the Sangha who practiced as couples. I wanted to find a way to transform this suffering, but I was not very skillful.

A couple of years passed. I went to retreats, I joined Thich Nhat Hanh and the Plum Village community in Vietnam; it was wonderful and still I had a deep longing to share these experiences with my partner. When I came home, I talked a lot about what happened, trying to draw him into what was so important to me. He listened and still made the choice not to join me at Sangha.

As my joy in the practice grew, so did my fears—fears that my partner and I were growing apart in our aspirations for how to live, and that this gap in our relationship would be hard to bridge.

One day, I was talking to a Sister at the Deer Park Monastery about my suffering. She listened deeply as I shared my feelings, and then she said, "Can you look deeply and see that his practice is to support you?"

Holding this question, I began to relax and connect with the wonderful ways my partner supported me. My heart opened and I experienced a softness that had been missing for a very long time. Until this moment, I hadn't been able to understand the root cause of my suffering. Now I was able to see my attachment to having him walk the path as I was walking it. And I was able to connect with my deep gratitude for his love and understanding of how important the practice was for me. And then a new question arose: How am I supporting him on his chosen path? This turned out to be the growing edge of practice that I brought with me to the Plum Village twenty-one-day retreat in France.

When I returned, I was truly interested in how his time had been in my absence, and I delighted in what he shared. I felt a real connection with his experiences even though I had not been present. And I realized that when I'd returned from retreats in the past, I'd talked a lot about my own experiences. This time, following the thread of his interests in the conversation, I shared only a few things with him. I continued to practice with the question, "How am I supporting my partner?"

A few weeks later, he asked me if I would be willing to do sitting meditation with him in the mornings. As we were both experiencing the shift in energy in our relationship and in our home, the opportunity to start our own Sangha presented itself. He was quite enthusiastic about this possibility. This was something he wanted us to share. Now the Sangha meets weekly in our home.

I have come to understand that loving my partner means supporting him as he finds his way in life. I continue to practice, staying aware of the suffering that comes when I hold ideas about how we should each walk in life. I continue to practice, determined not to water the seeds of attachment that are still present in me. I water the seeds of happiness that come with learning how to love my partner, aware that he is watering these same seeds.

PRACTICE: *A Time for Reflection*

+ Look deeply and recognize your own flowers—your virtues, kindness, talents, skillfulness.

+ Make a list of your happiness that is here and now in your daily life.

+ Look deeply into some of your challenges—your unhelpful habit energies. How do you get in your own way?

+ Look deeply into creative and concrete ways and practices you might use to transform your challenges.

+ Look deeply into the roots of our global challenges and reflect on what you can do to help the situation.

PART TWO

Loving Your Partner

CHAPTER FIVE

Watering Positive Seeds

For the more we are, the richer everything we experience is. And those who want to have a deep love in their lives must collect and save for it, and gather honey.

—Rainer Maria Rilke

WATERING SEEDS

We all have the potential to be full-time Buddhas; but most of us are only part-time, because we fall into forgetfulness. The practice of mindfulness is the practice of love. When we begin a relationship, there's a lot of energy to explore and a lot of excitement. But it takes time to know another person well. When we live with someone, often our initial projection of perfection will fall away and we will meet our real partner for the first time. Without the practice of mindfulness, it is difficult to make it through this normal and necessary part of the process of discovering true love.

We have looked at and explored practices to water the positive seeds in yourself. How can you water these seeds in your partner? Every time you can observe and nourish these positive seeds in your partner, you strengthen the bond between the two of you. This is not a short-term project! True love includes the sense of responsibility, accepting the other person as they are, with all their strengths and weaknesses. If we like only the best things in the person, that is not love. We have to accept the weaknesses and bring our patience, understanding, and energy to help them transform. The expression "long-term commitment" helps us understand the word love. In the context of true *love*, commitment can only be long-term. "I want to love you. I want to help you. I want to care for you. I want you to be happy. I want to work for happiness. But just for a few days." Does this make sense?

To begin, you may need to remember those positive seeds that you first noticed in your partner. How did you meet? At first, you might have just a one-sentence answer: "We met at work (or at the grocery store, or through online dating, or through a friend)." These one-line answers miss out on what gives each relationship its unique nature and energy. Every love story has a spark, otherwise your love would not have manifested. Retelling that story is a way to stir the embers and rekindle the spark.

Reflect on the story of your love. How did it come to pass that you met? What brought you to this moment in time? Here's our story.

"Today is the Epiphany! I propose we have a Renaissance festival!" Jean Houston proclaimed with all the gusto of a Shakespearean cheerleader. Jean was wearing a colorful Egyptian kaftan and her brown eyes were full of energy.

This was the first day of a three-year training program in human capacities, a school developed by Jean Houston and other remarkable teachers. We were in upstate New York in a summer camp gymnasium with 180 fellow classmates from fourteen countries.

Jean enthusiastically and quickly secured volunteers to coordinate various committees. The energy in the room was electric and folks were scurrying around like ants on assignment.

Peggy: *This sounds like fun, but I am too tired to join in the excitement. This is my first break from Doctoral studies and teaching in such a long time. I am glad that I am sitting in the back of the room. I want a nap.*

Larry: *I've just flown eight thousand miles from Hong Kong and climbed into a crowded rental car. It feels like the middle of the night to me. What am I doing in this place? I need some down time and some alone time and here I am in some sort of off-Broadway production effort. If I time it just right, I can sneak out the back door without being noticed.*

"That must be everything," Jean announced. We each separately breathed a sight of relief and were headed for the door when we heard her say, "You there, green jacket, you're Queen. Every Renaissance ball needs a Queen! You there, you are King!"

Peggy: *So much for lying low. I look to the King. Not a slip of a smile.*

Larry: *I don't want to be King at this moment. I don't even want to be here. I feel more like Scrooge. I move slowly, looking toward the Queen. She is beautiful, nervous, but seems willing to play her part.*

We exchanged a glance, and saw ourselves mirrored in each other's eyes briefly before being whisked away by our newly appointed "attendants" to get ready for the celebration.

We later entered the gymnasium to triumphant music. We were escorted to our thrones: two decorated folding chairs on a raised platform. Our attendants seated us, gave us food and drink, and then they left. We ate Greek olives, pita bread, and grapes. All community members presented themselves before us individually with a royal bow.

We had several hours sitting on our throne to get acquainted. Alone for the first time, coming from a place of doing too much, we were in total agreement about not wanting to be on stage. We both would have preferred to be followers rather than leaders. We exchanged stories about our lives. We listened well to each other and time passed quickly.

Late in the evening, Jean asked all of us to find a partner. We took each other's hand. At Jean's urging, we took our turns being a holy child and a holy elder who blesses the child, kneeling before one another and placing our hands on each other's head. Along with the initial sensation of physical contact was an electric charge that surprised and moved us. Even though we had only known each other for a few hours, we were both filled with an energy that we knew to be love.

Of course, having a beautiful moment of meeting didn't change the fact that our relationship, like most, had some major bumps along the way to our becoming a committed couple. Peggy was married to Steve and living in Vancouver, British Columbia, when we met. Larry was living in Hong Kong and married. In New York, we made a vow to become real and platonic friends and support each other's journey of transformation and healing. We saw each other a few times over four years as friends. Things changed. Larry divorced his wife, moved to Florida, and started new work in consulting. Steve and Peggy moved to Idaho. Then, Steve was killed in a skiing accident.

Several months after Steve's death, Peggy received an envelope with a tape from Larry. No note, just a tape. On the tape, he said he was speaking from a closet in a hotel room. Peggy remembers, "He was thinking of me and knew that I was suffering. He was trying to think what he could do to help and the only thing that came to him was to sing some songs that he knew I would enjoy. He sang gospel and show tunes. His voice was beautiful, but I was most touched by the image of him lying in a closet and wishing me well. About a year later, our simple friendship changed to a romantic relationship. Then I had to meet his family."

For Peggy, having grown up white in a white suburb, spending time in a city where she was the only white person in sight was challenging. "Larry's family welcomed me. Still, that first night, I went to bed feeling this whole thing had been a mistake. We were too different. I would wait until we were back in Idaho and then I would break up with Larry. I hoped we could be friends, but marriage was out of the question.

"The next morning I felt different. Although I had no recollection of a dream, I felt something had changed. I realized that Larry and I were more alike than we were different. With this realization, I was no longer afraid of our relationship. It was almost another year later, on Valentine's Day, when Larry bent down on one knee and proposed. He placed a ring on my finger. I heard the part of me that wanted to say no, and I listened and waited while I found the bigger part of me that wanted to say yes."

At least once a year, we tell each other this story of our meeting. This reminds us of what positive seeds we first noticed in each other and also helps stir the embers of that initial attraction.

PRACTICE: *Write Your Love Story*

Block out an hour or two of uninterrupted time. Have a pen and paper. You might find it useful to have some photo albums from the early stages of your relationship. How did you meet? What were your thoughts? Can you remember any specific details, like what you were wearing, what flowers were in bloom, what senses might be engaged. What was your courtship like? What was your journey of falling in love? What stars would you select to play your roles? Think about this love, how it came about, where it took place, what brought you to this moment in time. You can write this with your partner or write it separately and then share stories and see what different details emerge.

WATERING THE GOOD MEMORIES

As our relationships grow, more and more memories build up—good as well as difficult ones. Often in relationships we remember the difficult memories. We nurse perceived hurts and slights and give them disproportionate weight. One of the easiest ways to water the positive seeds in your partner is to spend some time recalling some of your happier moments together. What you pick as your happy memories may be different for each of you.

What we pay attention to has power. It's easy to fixate on something that is not working or to get stuck with something that annoys or frustrates us. When we are focused on how a person keeps the kitchen counters or manages the TV volume, it's easy to forget that our relationship is something nourishing that can water the best seeds within us.

Here are two of our good memories that we call on when we need this reminder.

Peggy's memory:

It is late at night and we are lost. Clouds blanket the stars. Larry is driving a friend's Volkswagen and I'm attempting to read the map. We're staying with friends in Seattle. There aren't many vehicles on the road on this dark winter night. City lights brighten the night sky.

"Do you have a favorite song?" I ask.

"Hmmmm, that's not so easy to pick a favorite," he says.

"Well, pick one and sing it to me. We can take turns."

Larry sings "Some Enchanted Evening." His rich voice fills the space. We go back and forth, laughing and singing and circling Seattle. Hymns, gospel, show tunes, camp songs, and more hymns. We laugh, we sing, and we drive in circles. We are lost. My eyes are wet with tears. We sing our way through Seattle and the thirty-minute drive takes us three hours. I do believe I now know all his favorite songs.

Larry's memory:

Our olive green corduroy couch is full of happy memories. We shopped around, looking for the perfect couch with a special purpose in mind. The idea was to find a couch where we could give each other foot rubs at the same time. The shopping experience was fun, as we had to try out couches until we found The Couch.

One day, we cotaught a seminar on diversity issues that was particularly wrought with challenges. This is often true of the first day of a seminar. I entered the house first, dropped my briefcase and collapsed into the couch. I was exhausted. Spent. Used up.

A few minutes later, Peggy settled into the other end of the sectional. She removed my socks and put my feet in her lap. She presented her feet to me. We were silent for the first five minutes. Rubbing, kneading, stroking. It felt good, really good to have my feet rubbed like this. And then something changed. I became aware that I was kneading, rubbing, and stroking the feet of my beloved. I lost track of whose feet were whose. I was overcome with love for toes, heels, and instep, these amazing feet. Whose amazing feet are these?

Recalling happy memories is one way of recognizing and communicating appreciation for the gifts and abilities of your partner. Be sincere: tell the truth using words and ideas that are comfortable for you. Keep it simple: over-praising can water down the impact. Be specific: the olive green of the couch, the song your partner was singing. Specificity builds confidence and will help you to communicate an idea clearly.

PRACTICE: *Remembering Magical Moments*

Block out an hour of uninterrupted time. Have pen and paper and/or art supplies handy. It might help to have some photo albums handy. Relax, breathe, rest. Enjoy 5–10 minutes of mindful breathing. Recall a time:

When you and your partner laughed and laughed …
When you felt deeply loved and loving …
When you felt attuned, understood, and appreciated …
When you couldn't keep your hands off each other …
When you lost track of time together …
When you shared a meaningful adventure …
When you discovered something new in each other …
When you felt lucky to be together …

Jot down some words or phrases that will help you recall this memory like: "David's birthday party," "our vacation on the coast," and so on.

Now, choose one memory that you are particularly drawn to. Settle into experiencing that one moment in time. Take your time. Bring this recollection into the present moment. What are you doing, seeing, hearing, smelling, and feeling? Take your time, tune in. Reach for a fast-writing pen and paper and write in the present tense, "I am," "we are," and write without editing. Go! It is helpful to do this with several memories so that you can remember this in your body and mind. Share your discoveries with your partner.

Enjoying Each Other

NORMA BRADLEY

Twenty years into our relationship, I was doing what I needed to do to create art and teach. One year, I was away from home for almost six months, returning only on weekends. My husband and I hardly had time to say hello before I was leaving for another project.

When I started to become aware that our relationship was withering like a flower, I recalled precious memories from the beginning of our relationship and realized that I was no longer taking care of our love. Jim and I talked about things that we enjoy and how we could again nurture precious time together.

First, I found a position where I could continue to create art and work in schools in my own community. A few years ago, Jim began playing the piano. I started taking voice lessons last year and now Jim accompanies me on the piano. Our relationship not only survived, but also flourished in a way I wouldn't have thought possible.

> *Nevertheless it means much to have loved, to have been happy, to have laid my hand on the living garden, even for one day.*
>
> —Jorge Luis Borges

THE ART OF ACKNOWLEDGMENT

It may seem obvious that we need to carve out time for recognition and appreciation of our partner, but we all have strong habit energy patterns in our culture and in ourselves that direct us to fill our time with work, shopping, children, anything and anyone but our romantic partner. In his book, *Bowling Alone: The Collapse and Revival of American Community*, Robert Putnam found that married partners engaged in an average of less than one hour a week of conversation.

A healthy relationship requires that we set aside time for it, just as our garden requires that we take the time to do the work it needs. And, just as there's no point in having a garden if we don't also take the time to sit and appreciate it, there is no point having a relationship if you don't spend time just appreciating the beautiful and positive seeds of your partner. As Thich Nhat Hanh writes, "Don't just hope for the other shore to come to you. If you want to cross over to the other shore, the shore of safety, well-being, non-fear, and non-anger, you have to swim or row across. You have to make an effort."

MESSENGERS OF LOVE

One way to acknowledge your partner is by giving him or her something tangible, such as a list or a letter. Letter writing is a form of speech. A letter can sometimes be safer than speaking because there is time for you to read what you have written before sending it. As you read your words, you can visualize the other person receiving your letter. As you write, consider if any phrase might be misunderstood or upsetting. If so, rewrite it. Remember both you and your partner will have these words on paper to refer to, so take the time to write exactly what you want to be remembered.

Make your letter as specific as possible. Here's an excerpt of a letter from Larry to Peggy:

Dearest Peggy,

When I was very young, I would sit in the attic of our house and look out at the stars at night and sing to myself. One song ended with the line that goes something like this: "When this life is through and the angels ask me to recall the thrill of them all, I will tell them it was my love for you."

Ten things I love about you:

1. That you instantly remember and always love my mother.
2. That you are graceful and easy for me to love.
3. Your willingness to travel to Cleveland with me; your open-heartedness and kindness to my family.

4. You introduced me to Thich Nhat Hanh and to this practice.

5. Your openness to your own creativity, gifts, and talents are a constant inspiration to me.

6. Your willingness to journey with me to a new land, a new life, leaving behind close friends and dear memories.

7. Your patience in putting up with lonely nights and days while I travel away from our new home.

8. Your unconditional love and support of our Sangha and its individual members.

9. Your visionary sense of our life together as a ministry to all beings.

10. Your true love in my life has supported and continues to support my transformation, healing, and journey home to my self.

With my whole life I love you.

If writing is not a natural way for you to communicate, there are plenty of other, nonverbal, tangible ways to express your love. Our friend, Tracy, recommends placing an empty vase in a visible spot in your house. Either person in the relationship can place a flower in that vase when they want to communicate something to the other partner, whether that something is "I'm sorry" or "I love you." This is a quiet way of expressing your love to your partner that does not require that they respond before they are ready to do so.

In Myrlie Evers's autobiography entitled *Watch Me Fly*, she speaks of her life and love of civil rights leader Medgar Evers. Here is her story of a quiet message of love:

I love roses, but Medgar could never afford to buy me a florist's bouquet. So he did something better. Every year, he made a ritual of giving me bare-root roses to plant in our yard, and eventually, three dozen rose bushes were the envy of our neighbours. Once in awhile, Medgar would gather a bouquet, or perhaps just one rose, and hand it to me as he came through the door. It became an unspoken verse of the love between us.

Peggy's parents liked to play special songs for heart to heart communication. Harry Belafonte meant one thing, while Dave Brubeck communicated another message. Our sister, Kay, is a lover of doughnuts and a good cup of coffee. Her husband, Mike, enjoys bringing her a fresh cup of java and waving it under her nose as she is first awakening, and doughnuts often receive a special presentational flair. What memories do you have of symbols, sounds or images that speak to you of your love for your partner?

PRACTICE: *Memories of Unspoken Verses of Love*

+ Find a quiet place for peaceful reflection. Have writing and/or art supplies nearby.
+ Enjoy mindful breathing to gently and naturally

restore peace to your body and mind. Rest comfortably. Enjoy 5–10 minutes of mindful breathing.

+ Now select as an object of meditation the memory of unspoken verses of love. Is there a symbol of unspoken love that arises?

+ Is there something that sparks your wedding vow, your commitment to love, and the face of your beloved? Is there a sound, song, or musical memory?

+ Is there a taste, smell, or aroma? Is there a texture, sensation, or touch? What images and symbols come to mind?

+ At the end of your meditation, you can either journal or draw some of the images, symbols, experiences, and memories that communicate to you your love for your partner.

CREATING A SHARED PRACTICE

Perhaps you have already created a practice that communicates "I love you" to your partner. If you have, it is a good thing to talk about this with your partner so that your understanding of this tool can deepen.

To create your own practice set aside some time to talk to your partner about how to establish a symbol that communicates "I love you" or "I am thinking of you and sending my love." It helps to choose something that is easy to access and readily available and that has depth and potency for both of you.

DATES TO DO NOTHING

One of the advantages of the flower vase or the love letter is that they can be done anytime, even in the midst of a busy day. Ideally, along with these affirmations of love, you and your partner can create some structured time to water the positive seeds in each other. For many of us, it takes a lot of effort to set up this time. Whether it's hiring a babysitter, getting a reservation at the right restaurant, or getting dressed up, we often feel we don't have the time or energy to do something special or have a "date" once we are in a committed relationship with a partner. Our dates get fewer and farther between, we feel we have to make an even bigger effort, and we put it off even further.

Instead of a formal date, or even the standard dinner and a movie, we recommend scheduling what Thich Nhat Hanh calls a "lazy day" together. Plum Village, where Thich Nhat Hanh lives, describes a lazy day as a day for us to be truly with the day, without having any scheduled activities. We just let the day unfold naturally, timelessly. It is a day in which we can practice as we like. We may do walking meditation on our own or with a friend or do sitting meditation in the forest. We might like to read lightly or write home to our family or to a friend. It can be a day for us to look deeper at our practice and at our relations with others. On this day, we have a chance to balance ourselves.

Lazy isn't about going to sleep. It isn't about goofing off or zoning out. Lazy is more about creating a relaxed and easy quality to being with your partner. Having lazy time with yourself and your partner is about time that isn't busy, scheduled, over-filled with people, places, and activities. It's about stopping and entering into the speed of life.

When you combine the idea of a lazy day with watering the positive seeds in your partner, you get something our friend Suzanne calls "wooing time." This is her expression for a block of daytime carved out to be alone with her husband. Her teenage son knows to be out with his friends; their friends know not to stop by; they put a DO NOT DISTURB sign on the door; they take their phone off the hook, and the turn off computer. Sometimes they take a walk, but generally they stay home—in their bedroom, hot tub, living room, or garden. "Just us chickens," she likes to say. Suzanne and Calvin set aside almost every Saturday for wooing time.

There is nourishment in just stopping. Then there is the added practice of calming and relaxing, of having nothing to do and nowhere to go. For wooing time to be successful, you will need to do artful management of your boundaries. These boundaries are connected to your physical space, your relationships with others, and your time and technology. It will help to make childcare or other agreements ahead of time and discuss what your rules will be for this wooing time. We like to have a no-cars and no-technology rule to help us stop, relax, and rest with one another. We plan ahead and discuss any meals and meal preparation so that we know what tasks and activities might be a part of this time.

THE FRUIT OF WATERING
POSITIVE SEEDS

We have all experienced moments in time when we were caught by beauty. Whether it was a passing glance at an intricate web of a spider, the song of a lark, the rays of the sun on the sunflowers, or a grin on a dog's face. This is the practice of mindfulness and attention. Through our practice of mindfulness, we have the opportunity to have more of these moments, as life is always available and magic is ever underfoot. It is we that stray from the kingdom. Through conscious breathing we can be with life as it is—and it is a marvel!

We all have had moments when we just happen to look at our partner and with that glance we cut through eternity. Our heart is penetrated with love as we experience our partner deeply. It might just be a simple gesture, a soft smile or a few words that catch our attention, but we find our reality cut through with brilliance as we behold the wonder that is our partner. She is so lovely. He is so kind. She is so talented. He is a wonder. And this is the truth. Our partner is a wonder. We are a wonder.

Life is new and complete in each moment. And yet we often find ourselves missing this moment, rushing to be somewhere else. We often rush to get to where we are going and don't settle in before we are rushing off to our next meeting. We can worry about the past or plan for the future and totally miss this moment and being with what or who is in front of us.

Try this with your partner. Say "I am here, I am present, I am available" and truly be there. What do you notice? Mindfulness is the energy that helps us to recognize each other. We are miracles gazing at miracles.

CHAPTER SIX

Offerings

A family is a place where minds come in contact with one another. If these minds love one another, the home will be as beautiful as a flower garden. But if these minds get out of harmony with one another, it is like a storm that plays havoc with the garden.

—The Buddha

When we're upset with someone, we have a tendency to punish him or her. We do this in many ways: sometimes by withholding attention, sometimes by withholding words. This only escalates our own suffering. Withholding water doesn't help a garden grow and withholding our attention and love will not help our relationship flower.

The more we water the positive seeds in our partner, the more we ourselves grow, and the more our feeling of spiritual wealth and our capacity for generosity increase. In Buddhist teachings, the practice of giving is referred to as transcendent generosity, the first of the six *paramitas* or perfections. The others are: virtue, patience, effort, meditation, and wisdom.

The practice of generosity can be the first step in restoring a relationship. Generosity involves the power of surrender, of letting go. There is a well-known plant in Vietnam called *he* (pronounced "hay") that's a member of the onion family. This plant is delicious in soup, fried rice, and in omelettes. It grows back in less than twenty-four hours after it's cut. The more you cut this plant, the bigger and stronger it becomes. The paramita of generosity is like this. When we give freely, we receive freely and fully.

The Buddha advised us that it's not possible to live a spiritual life without a generous heart. A true gift is always given in the spirit of understanding and with no expectation of receiving anything in return. It's given with no hidden agenda and no aim of trying to win someone over. There's no discrimination between the one who gives and the one who receives. When you see that people need help, you offer and share what you have, as naturally as you breathe.

We often think of gifts as material objects—a book, a homemade painting, or a bowl of soup. But as well as material things, we can give the gift of our time, our presence, our attention, and our example, providing a refuge for those who need a place of safety and being fully present where there is darkness and suffering.

You don't need to wait until a holiday or anniversary to give one of these gifts to your partner. These offerings are always available to give, and each one, no matter how small, adds strength to your relationship. When we're angry with our partner, giving them a gift can break through our feelings of resentment and open the way for love and communication to flow again. It can be a good idea to buy or make something in advance. Then we are always ready when such a time arrives.

THE GIFT OF TEA

There is a Japanese saying that is used as part of a tea ceremony: "Ichi go ichi e." This can be translated as "One lifetime, one meeting." Every meeting we have happens only once in a lifetime. Meeting each moment with this attitude is meeting with the Buddha or with the divine aspect present in the moment and in us. Each moment is new and complete and it will never happen again.

Taking the time to pour tea, or another offering that you and your partner enjoy, is a way of offering the gift of time to your beloved. It's important that you choose something that's simply prepared and easy to enjoy. You can just sit quietly with your partner, enjoying each other's company and your drink.

Give a Gift of Tea

CAROLYN MARSDEN

I've taken the Buddha's practice of giving a gift to heart—I find it especially useful when I'm arguing with my husband. When I am upset with my husband, I make myself leave the scene as quickly as I can. Inevitably, my ego demands that I re-enter the fray to prove my husband wrong—he must admit I'm right and apologize!

Instead, I collect myself and return to my breath. My husband loves tea, and he loves it prepared a certain way. I take great care to mindfully prepare and serve a beautiful cup of tea. I find that focusing on the cup, the water, the tea leaves, the sound of the water pouring into the cup, the feel of my hands on the kettle, all of this brings me back to myself. I come home, I remember who I am and what is important. Sometimes I prepare a cup for myself and do so with this same loving attention. I see this cup of tea as a symbol of my love and friendship.

I take the tea, set it down next to him, and either sit or leave without saying a word. Offering the tea is a kind of bowing down, a touching of the earth. If we do speak about the argument, it is when we are calmer and clearer. Often, though, neither of us feels the need to bring it up even though it seemed all-consuming at that time.

A few weeks ago this practice stood me in good stead. I opened up a piece of mail with Dutch stamps addressed to my husband—I thought it was junk mail. It turned out to be a cargo invoice for a vehicle shipped from Holland. I ran upstairs shouting, "You didn't buy a car, did you?" He had indeed. Our finances were in ruins. We couldn't afford a car. I later learned that the car was not on its way to the U.S., but to Belize, the destination of a surprise trip he was planning for us. He planned that we would drive it back afterward.

I didn't bring my husband that cup of tea as quickly as I normally would. It took several days before I finally began to understand what in my husband had led him to buy this car. I witnessed his regret. When I could finally let go of the need to be in control, I was able to bring him that cup of tea. I even added honey.

THE GIFT OF SPACE

When we think of giving the gift of ourselves to a person, we often think of moving closer to them. But for a relationship to thrive, one of the best gifts we can give our partner is space.

When Peggy studied floral design, she made a mistake commonly made by new designers. She used too many flowers and pushed them too firmly into the container. Her teacher would study the arrangements she'd made, viewing them from all sides. Then he'd remove some of the flowers and greenery. And finally, he'd pull the remaining flowers and greenery up and out, creating more height and, most importantly, more space. Each flower needs space around it so it can radiate its own beauty.

Human beings are like flowers. We, too, need space around us to exist and for our beauty and presence to manifest in the world. The sensation of needing or wanting more space is a bell of mindfulness. Without space within us and around us, we can't be happy. Often, our first tendency is to be annoyed with our partner and feel the urge to run away. We once saw a cartoon that showed two people in a restaurant—a woman and what appeared to be a man in an astronaut's suit. They'd been served dinner and the woman was looking at the face of the man in the astronaut's suit. He was saying to her, "I think I need a little more space."

Make a commitment to support your partner in cultivating spaciousness. The human heart can operate like a big magnet; we want to possess things and persons, and we don't want to experience being separated from someone we love. We believe that we're dependent on their presence for our happiness, and in doing so we lose our freedom and threaten theirs. We're stuck. We believe our happiness is conditional, dependent on us being attached to this other person.

Nonattachment is hard! It's counterintuitive to a lot of things we've been taught and believe. Without practice, it's impossible to give ourselves and our partner the space we need to thrive. You might practice this first with something other than a person—perhaps with a pet, a special plant, your favorite pen, the first cup of coffee of the day, or a treasured tool or piece of clothing.

First, say its name and imagine that you are speaking to it. "Yes, you are precious and important to me. I care about you. But no matter how much I care for you and love you, you are not my life. You are not essential for my life. I let you go."

Once you have tried this with an inanimate object, practice with your attachment to another person. Say the name of someone you feel attached to. Picture them smiling at you with love. You might imagine holding their hands as you say, "Yes [say their name], I love you. You are precious and important to me, and you are not my life. I love you and I let you go." Surprise! When you can say this and really mean it, you will experience greater closeness.

THE GIFT OF NO FEAR

According to the Buddha, the greatest gift we can give is the gift of no fear. Practicing meditation, we come to see that we "inter-are" with all other beings. With that understanding, our fears, anxieties, anger, and sorrow disappear. We're in touch with things as they are and we've transcended all notions of permanence, of self, and of birth and death. When we're able to touch the ultimate dimension in ourselves and in everything, we no longer feel fear.

To see how you can give the gift of no fear in your relationship, it may be helpful to think of one person who has given you this gift. For Peggy, it's her grandmother:

My Grandma Dunn liked to dress well, smoke Pall Mall straights, and speak her mind. She and my grandfather had big plans for his retirement, including travel and regular visits to their cabin in northern Wisconsin. A week after his retirement, my grandfather died. About a month after the funeral, Grandma was visiting. She was busy writing at the dining room table, and from time to time she'd sigh and make a trip to the kitchen for iced tea.

I asked, "What are you writing about?"

"I'm making a list," she said. She looked up from her paper and met my gaze. I watched her eyes soften. "We had our life all planned out." She said, "And I have to make some new plans. I'm not happy about this, but it is what I have to do. I'm not fixing to die anytime soon, and I have some living to do. I'm making a Life List."

"Can I see what's on the list?" I asked. She smiled and said, "Sit down next to me and see what you think." She handed me the list. I read aloud: "(1) Sell everything; (2) Meet the Pope; (3) Go to the Holy land;

(4) Travel to Egypt and climb the pyramids; (5) Learn flamenco dancing; (6) Find wonderful friends who love to play bridge; (6) Visit the three best shelling beaches; (7) Spend time with my family and friends; (8) Stay healthy; and (9) Have fun."

"This is my last go-round," she said. "I'm living it for all it's worth." And that's what she did.

She sold her homes and most of her possessions and bought a one-way ticket to Rome. She put on her peacock-blue suit and black lace mantilla and went to the Vatican. She was directed to the papal office where she was asked if she had an appointment. "No, but I'm sure that he is expecting me," she said. And sure enough, in about an hour, she met with Pope John Paul I. From here she began her journey.

After living in Spain, playing bridge, traveling, and dancing for several years, she returned home to Wisconsin. Flat broke, she promptly put on her pea-cock-blue suit, kid gloves, and hat and went to apply at Smartwear, a Milwaukee department store. She was hired that day to manage the children's department.

When my husband, Steve, was killed, I was heart-broken and angry. And I remembered my grandmother and her Life List. I sat down and made my list to remind myself that I had a whole lot of living left to do.

What does it mean to give the gift of no fear? We read a story about a family with a ten-year-old son in need of a blood transfusion and bone marrow transplant. The six-year-old daughter in the family happened to meet the requirements and was the only possible donor that the family could find. The doctor asked the little girl if she would give her blood and bone marrow to help her brother. The girl took some time to think about it. Later that day, she told the doctor that she would be okay with having the procedure.

The next day she was brought into the hospital and put on a cart next to her brother. The doctor came up to her as they were setting up the equipment.

"Doctor," she said, "will it hurt to die?" She had not understood the procedure and thought that she would have to die to save her brother. This is the gift of no fear.

In the early nineties, Thich Nhat Hanh's monastery in France, Plum Village, was famous for its fleet of broken-down automobiles. Any spare dollar was going to Vietnam, so the cars were held together with band-aids, duct tape, and prayer. And, of course, they were always breaking down.

One day, someone donated an almost new Mercedes Benz. Thich Nhat Hanh immediately asked to have it traded in for multiple vehicles. The working Mercedes was converted into six vehicles that sometimes worked. Larry ran into Sister Chan Khong, Thich Nhat Hanh's longtime student and assistant, and asked if having the cars breaking down was upsetting to Thay. (Thay means "teacher" in Vietnamese and is what Thich Nhat Hanh's students call him.) She said, "Oh, no, it's just an opportunity for him to enjoy walking meditation."

Another time we were having tea with Thich Nhat Hanh when he received the news that a family member in Vietnam had passed over. At that time, he was not allowed to enter Vietnam. Immediately, he stood up and practiced walking meditation. When he returned to tea, he was at peace. Witnessing our teacher handle the big and small storms of everyday life in this way has taught us to move directly into walking meditation when we are experiencing a flood of emotions. Our teacher taught us you could give the gift of no fear to your partner just by practicing it.

PRACTICE: *A Teacher of No Fear*

+ Set aside a window of quiet time with your partner. Have your journal and art supplies handy. Begin by breathing and coming home to yourself.

+ Then reflect on the question: who has been a teacher of no fear? Recall some of the faces, smiles, memories, feelings connected with your teachers of no fear. Choose one that you are particularly drawn to today.

+ Focus on this teacher of no fear. What did they teach you about love? How is this person alive in you today?

+ At the end of your meditation time, pick up your journal and/or art supplies. You might want to draw a picture of this teacher, or write a thank you letter to the teacher of no fear.

+ Share your reflections with your partner. Thank each
other for sharing these stories and then share with
your partner how you experience their teacher of no
fear as present and alive in their life and actions.

PRACTICE: *No Fear*

The gift of no fear is a wonderful gift. Your understanding of
this gift will grow out of your practice of mindfulness, concentration and insight. Here are some journal topics that will help
you deepen your insight and practice of no fear.

+ What does it mean to give the gift of no fear?
+ Write about a time when you resisted criticizing,
punishing or blaming your partner and instead
offered love.
+ Write about your journey of growing faith in your
relationship.
+ Write about a time when you were fearless with
your love.

CHAPTER SEVEN

Taking Refuge

🌿

Today, today, today ... bless us
and help us to grow
—from the Rosh Hashanah Liturgy

The garden is always poised to offer a lesson on love. A relationship with the entire cosmos is so evident in the garden. The dew kissed grass, the artwork of spiders, the hum of ecosystems are brimming with life in the garden. God's voice is heard, felt, tasted in the garden. Who grew the flower? Who invited the rain?

True love, whether it is romantic, brotherly, or for humanity, transcends the physical realm. It is more than a feeling. It is an infinite force of light and of love that speaks of our interconnectedness with all things. We remember that God is in partnership with us. This is stabilizing, invigorating, and life giving. When a couple invites the Beloved to be a part of their relationship, then love becomes unbounded. Love is not focused on another person, or set up with contingencies about having a certain experience, or behaving in a certain way. The relationship, like the garden, has different seasons of unfolding through cycles of birth and death. Our resistance, fear, hurt, and anger become compost that becomes new flowers. Our weeds teach us about intimacy.

Then there are those moments when we feel isolated or disconnected from our partner. Moments when our energy, joy and enchantment are missing. We remind ourselves that this is a sign that we are disconnected from ourselves and from spirit. We remember that we have invited the divine into our life and our home and we call on the divine aspect within us and amongst us. And all will be well as it always is.

We wrote to our friends John and Susan Turner, who have been married for over thirty years, and asked them the secret to their marital happiness. This is what they said: "Spiritual practice has been a cornerstone of our daily life, and it has evolved and deepened over the years. We consult God in all that we do and always honor the Divine in each other. Our partnership has gone beyond explanation."

Watering the positive seeds in your partner is the beginning. Offering the gifts of time, space, understanding, and no fear will ensure your relationship has rich and fertile soil to work with. But it is through creating routines and rituals that the spiritual component of your relationship deepens and strengthens and creates a love that is indestructible.

MAKING LOVE VISIBLE

Take a moment to reflect on the most recent wedding you have attended. What do you remember from the ceremony? Often, the vows are the most emotionally and spiritually binding part of the ceremony. Vows make our love visible. They are drawn from the heart and they speak to the heart. They are a public proclamation of love and they offer a blueprint for your future as a couple.

Conscious commitment has a life giving quality. A conscious commitment is not a marriage out of duty, or some kind of glue that we share so we can stick something out. This commitment is to create, nourish, and cultivate a healthy, fresh, kicking life-giving partnership that provides inspiration to the world.

If you have written vows for your relationship, take a look at them and see if they still have a charge, a light and positive energy for you. If they do, frame them and keep them on your family altar. If you would like to update them, we have a practice for you.

Vows are more than just a pretty speech. They are heart-felt spoken promises. As you speak these words, you make yourself accountable through intention—to yourself and to your beloved—to live, love and behave in a certain specified way. These vows can call us into our own greatness. They are a precious part of our annual renewal as a couple. We read our vows to each other as part of our annual beginning anew. We turn directly toward each other, face to face and we share our promises. This soul to soul encounter stirs the embers of our fire of love.

LARRY'S VOWS TO PEGGY

I promise you Peggy that I will:

Practice peace. I will honor you, listen to you and communicate whole heartedly with you.

Nurture and celebrate the treasured memories of John, Steve, Kathy and Viola as special ancestors in our family.

Look at you every day and smile with eyes of love and a heart full of trust.

Express with my own voice my dreams, emotions, difficulties and wonders.

Support and encourage you to live your spiritual and professional dreams.

Give you the space and time that you need to come home to your deepest self.

Water your flower everyday, so it may grow in our marriage, the flower of your intellect, the flower of your compassion, the flower of your beauty, the flower of your generosity and the flower of your originality.

Become more and more at ease and at home with myself in our relationship, to grow beyond my habits of distance and seriousness and become fuller of light and laughter.

Water my own flower through taking care of myself physically, emotionally, mentally and spiritually so that I can bring vitality and charm to the wonderful mystery of our marriage.

Sing, dance and make merry, to take great joy in the simple things that make us whole.

CREATING A SACRED SPACE

Every home in Vietnam and other Asian and African countries has an altar for ancestors. On the altar are pictures of ancestors who have passed away, or perhaps only one picture of an ancestor who represents all the ancestors; it may be the grandmother or the grandfather. Each morning someone wipes away the dust that might have gathered on the altar, lights a stick of incense, and bows. The incense is an offering to the ancestors.

In all of the homes we've had, we've made a practice space with a simple altar. Sometimes we've been lucky enough to have an entire room dedicated to our meditation and spiritual life. At other times we've only had space for a "breathing corner." The altar can be very small and simple. When we lived at Deer Park Monastery, we lived in one room. Our ancestral altar was on the top of a bookshelf. In our current home, we have a built-in cabinet with glass doors in our meditation room; the altar is in the cabinet.

There are many advantages to having a space dedicated to spiritual practice. First, it's practical. Having your chair or cushion ready to go makes it easy to add sitting meditation and other practices to your life, like settling into five minutes of mindful sitting before you walk out the front door to work or school. Having a spiritual center is also a reminder of your intention and commitment to your partner, family, and the world. Not only will this room or corner contribute positive energy to your home, this energy will also spill over into the world.

It's in this space that you can do much of your watering–seeds practice. It is here you may want to write your love letter to your partner. It's here you may want to retreat when you're giving your partner the gift of space.

THE FIVE AWARENESSES

One key ritual we recommend practicing in your spiritual space is reciting the Five Awarenesses. The Five Awarenesses are a part of the wedding ceremony in the tradition of Thich Nhat Hanh. We repeat them each month at the full moon as well as on our anniversary. Larry also includes the Five Awarenesses in his morning practice. And in sitting meditation, you can choose one or more of the awarenesses to use as the object of your meditation. We know some families that choose to repeat them with their children each week.

We discover that there is less "I-making'" when we remember that we are our ancestors and future generations. All of our actions are both mine and theirs, and our practice is for them. We want to do them proud! We are reminded of the great support that is available for us by our ancestors and the beautiful solid root that afford us stability, freedom, and beauty. We appreciate being reminded that blaming and arguing don't work and that understanding is the key to love.

The Five Awarenesses

(from *Chanting from the Heart*, Thich Nhat Hanh, Parallax Press, 2007)

THE FIRST AWARENESS

We are aware that all generations of our ancestors and all future generations are present in us.

THE SECOND AWARENESS

We are aware of the expectations that our ancestors, our children, and their children have of us.

THE THIRD AWARENESS

We are aware that our joy, peace, freedom, and harmony are the joy, peace, freedom, and harmony of our ancestors, our children, and their children.

THE FOURTH AWARENESS

We are aware that understanding is the very foundation of love.

THE FIFTH AWARENESS

We are aware that blaming and arguing can never help us and only create a wider gap between us—that only understanding, trust, and love can help us change and grow.

The Sun Room

PATRICIA WEBB AND DAVID MCCLESKEY

Our first meditation group was a Sangha of two. We made an altar in the living room where we practiced. We did walking meditation around the old Presbyterian Church across the street.

These days we have a Sangha of about fifteen who sit weekly in a large and lovely room in a nearby dojo. Witnessing the unfolding of this community has been a beautiful reminder of the fruits of the practice. We love each member and the whole of it with all our hearts, yet we still love to practice daily at home.

One of the best decisions we made when we moved into our small, second-floor apartment two years ago was to dedicate one of its four rooms to meditation. The Sun Room contains an altar with fresh flowers, a candle, a bell, and a statue of Avalokita. It's the smallest and most uncluttered room in our home. Two of the walls are windows, putting us in the treetops and giving us a chance to commune with the natural light at all times of day, in all seasons of the year. A picture of Thich Nhat Hanh, a William Blake quote, and a drum hang on the other two walls. It's hard to explain the spaciousness we experience in this small room devoted entirely to breathing. No matter how busy our schedules, the day begins here. We sit, breathe, journal, or give ourselves to silence. The energy that emanates from the Sun Room nourishes us twenty-four hours a day, its nurturing power permeating our home, breathing our intention like the heart and lungs of our relationship.

When we have a decision to make or an issue to resolve, we gravitate to the Sun Room. The energy field created by hours of sitting lends peace to the moment. We are often aware of how the Sun Room goes with us to work on challenging days or even on trips. We'll be moving soon. Will there be a room in the new place just for our daily practice? You bet!

> *Whose hands are these*
> *that have never died?*
> *Who is it who was born in the past?*
> *Who is it who will die in the future?*
>
> —Thich Nhat Hanh

MEETING THE FAMILY

Another key spiritual practice is to introduce your partner to your family, not only to your current family, but also to your ancestors. Take turns telling stories about your ancestors. Show each other pictures. You may want to engage in a practice called "Whose Hand Is This?"

If you look deeply into the palm of your hand, you will see your parents and grandparents.

A few years ago, we watched Michael Jordan receive an Image Award from the NAACP. He began his acceptance speech by thanking his father. He said that he wished his father was still here to be a part of receiving this award, as his gratitude to his father was immense. His eyes filled with tears, and he looked down at his hands for a few moments. He then looked up and raised his large graceful hands and faced his palms toward the audience and said, "Oh, my father is here. I am so glad." All of us who witnessed this moment were aware that Michael's father was present in him. We knew that they both were receiving the award.

It's possible to see all generations of ancestors in your palm. All of them are alive in this moment. Previous generations, all the way back to single-celled beings, are present in your hand. Look at your partner's hand. You'll see all of his or her ancestors there. When you create a spiritual space for yourself and your partner, you're creating a space for all your ancestors, past, present, and future.

The strength of your feelings is only one of the strands of that web. Supported by many elements, the couple will be solid, like a tree. To be strong, a tree sends more than one root deep into the soil. If a tree has only one root, it may be blown over by the wind.

On your altar, pictures of friends and loved ones past on and still living will remind you to practice your relationship in the context of a community. If you practice in this spirit, your wedding ring will become the ring of interbeing, of solidarity, of love and understanding.

DO YOU KNOW YOUR PARTNER'S BABY FACE?

On our family altar you will find framed pictures of ourselves at the age of five. We enjoy looking into each other's faces and discovering the baby face and have made it a regular practice. Seeing each other as a child now comes naturally. The happy child is easy to recognize at the beach, singing, and when we are enjoying each other. We have also come to value and love the sad, scared, confused, and angry little child when we experience stress or strife in our relationship. It is much easier to love when you remember that little boy or girl, and so much harder to stay angry.

At first we made the following meditation a regular practice. We have also used it "on the spot" when we have experienced upset with the other. By practicing these meditations regularly, the likelihood of them kicking in spontaneously is magnified. By making them a practice and by using them as a regular practice, then our unconscious will help us out. A wise voice will remind us that our partner is a miracle.

PRACTICE: *Guided Meditation* *Seeing Our Partner Five Years Old*

Settle into a quiet place where you can experience calm and ease. You can have this book handy and use this as a guide. We begin by breathing and settling. Allow a few minutes with each of the phrases.

Breathing in, know that you are breathing in. Breathing out, know that you are breathing out. Follow your in-breath all the way, follow your out-breath all the way. In. Out.

Breathing in, become aware of your whole body. Breathing out, relax your whole body. Breathing in, aware of body. Breathing out, relaxing. Body. Relaxing.

Breathing in, experience calm in your body. Breathing out, experience ease in your body. Breathing in, calm. Breathing out, ease.

Breathing in, see yourself as a five-year-old little boy or little girl, fragile and vulnerable. See or imagine this child standing in front of you. Breathing out, smile to the little fiveyear-old. See or imagine holding the hands of the little child. Breathing in, seeing yourself five years old. Breathing out, smiling to yourself as a five-year-old.

Breathing in, becoming aware that the five-year-old little boy or little girl is in you. Breathing out, loving and holding the five-year-old in you. Loving and holding the five-year-old child.

Breathing in, seeing your partner as a five-year-old little boy or little girl, fragile and vulnerable. Breathing out, smiling to your partner as a five-year-old child. See or imagine holding the hands of your partner. See your partner as a five-year-old child. Holding your partner's small hands.

Breathing in, becoming aware that your partner is in you, breathing out, holding your partner in you tenderly. Aware that your partner is in you. Holding your partner tenderly.

A Grandmother's Love

JAYNA GIEBER

I was flooded with grief. All of my memories of despair were devouring me—all of them consuming my heart and mind. I had a baby who died, I had lived through cancer, rape, addiction and my mother's death. This dark night, I crumpled to the floor and pulled my legs up into my chest to calm the shaking of my body.

My husband Jon came into the room and quietly asked how he could help.

"Nobody can help me but my grandmother. Only my grandmother would know how to comfort and hold me." I cried, gasping for breath with deep tears bubbling up from my belly. "She was the only one and she is not here. No one can help me."

I made myself into a tight little ball and rocked, holding on for what felt like dear life. I heard a sound behind me. Too weak to look, I waited, and heard footsteps drawing near. I felt a warm breath at my ear. "I'll be your grandma, little one. I'll take care of you. I love you. I am here," whispered the creaky voice.

I turned and saw a beautiful old grandmother cloaked in a deep purple shawl. I knew the caressing touch of the large work-worn hands on my shoulders. As my vision adjusted, I recognized the wrinkles around the warm brown eyes that were looking at me so kindly. From under the purple cloak, my husband's bearded face was smiling at me with pure love and acceptance. He opened the shawl wide, folded me into his arms and cradled my body.

Jon understood my deep longing for nurturing and acceptance in the face of great sorrow and confusion. Out of compassion for me, he was willing to be vulnerable, offering me his intimate and playful care. He had listened to me, looked deeply, and responded to what he heard with an open heart.

I wiggled my head out from under the shawl to take another incredulous look at my two hundred-pound, six-foot tall husband, his big furry face draped with the purple afghan my grandmother had crocheted, and I laughed and cried. My husband and my grandmother held me fiercely, and we both joined in laughter and tears.

The Dharma Is Bigger Than Us

CAROL LEELA VERITY

Maurice and I have been married for twenty years. We have seen our relationship go through many changes. The transformation in our relationship can be attributed to spiritual teachings and spiritual practice. The Dharma is bigger than us. When things have threatened our relationship, the teachings are here shining a guiding light, giving us clarity and wisdom on how to move forward. The teachings have been a strong unifying factor in our relationship. They enable us to put ourselves aside in the knowing that if we pay heed to the teachings, this is the best possible guidance. It takes time to trust oneself, it takes time to know that you will think and act in the best way. Mostly we don't even know what is the best way. Fortunately, we can place our unfailing trust in the Dharma to guide us until we fully embody its wisdom. For this I am grateful, and I look forward to our relationship growing more solidly as we continue to move through this life together.

CHAPTER EIGHT

Afflictions

🌿

Our greatest duty and our main duty is to help others. And please, if you can't help them, would you please not hurt them?

—The Dalai Lama

No matter how much we water our garden, no matter how fertile the soil, there will be weeds and pests. This is the nature of gardens. There might be moments when the relationship seems doomed to failure. This is because it takes practice to live fully in the present. We bring to a relationship all our old hurts and preconceptions from the past—our troubles, our afflictions—as well as unspoken hopes and dreams.

For Peggy, the honeymoon was a teachable moment:

The aquamarine waters shimmered against a cloudless blue sky. The warm sun kissed my face as I followed the shoreline, slowly walking as the foam tickled my ankles. The weather was perfect; our hotel room was spectacular. This was the first day of our honeymoon in Mexico, one of my favorite places in the world, and I was miserable.

I walked back to our room and Larry was still sleeping. We had arrived in the later afternoon and had gone to bed exhausted. It wasn't the classic honeymoon night, but we had our whole lives, right?

Larry looked at me with half-closed eyes. "Are you up for some breakfast?" I asked. I received a groan as he rolled over and went back to sleep.

OK, I thought. There was a sign in the lobby for a yoga class, so I made my way to the fitness center. While in the relaxation pose at the close of the class, I started crying. Not the big sobs, just tears that happened on their own, washing my face. I breathed into the sadness and just held myself.

After class, I went up to our room. I opened the door and the room was dark. Larry had pulled the two sets of shades and turned the room into a sleep cavern. This time he didn't wake up. I put my swimming suit on, grabbed a book and towels and went back to the beach.

The ocean water was warm and inviting. I dove in and spent hours floating and bobbing in the waves. From time to time my mind interrupted: Where's Larry? This is our honeymoon! I pictured Bert Lancaster and Ada Gardner in the movie *From Here to Eternity*, I should have married Bert Lancaster. At least he likes to swim.

When I returned to the room, the curtains were open and the sun was pouring in. No Larry. I took the elevator down to the restaurant on the first floor. There he was, eating eggs, reading the paper, bumpy hair and a four o'clock shadow. In fact, it WAS four o'clock.

"Good morning," I said with a smile.

"Ruugghh," he said as he made brief eye contact with me and went back to reading the newspaper.

I sat down and stared at the paper, trying to bore a hole through the other side. I went from sad to hurt to mad. Where was he? This was our honeymoon?

"What would you like to do today?" I asked hopefully.

"Sleep" he said. And his body language seemed to indicate he was saying, "Be alone."

I stood up and he looked up over the top of the paper. "Where are you going?" He asked.

"Well, it seems to me that you are wanting to be alone." I said.

"What makes you say that?" he asked.

"You seem more interested in the news than in me. You've hardly looked at me."

"Hey, I'm just waking up. I'm tired. What do you expect?"

"Oh, I just thought we might do something together," I said.

"Not today," he said, turning back to the paper.

I got up and propelled myself out of the restaurant and toward the beach. I felt heat in my belly and warm tears on my face. I practically ran into my yoga instructor. "Hola, Peggy," she said. And then she looked at my face. "Is everything OK?" I burst into tears. Through my tears and the "uh-uh" sounds that can happen when you are trying to talk and cry at the same time, I said something like, "He is tired and eating eggs and wants to be alone".

She looked at me kindly and said, "Yes, marriage is a dance." Something shifted: I could see many ages of me. The young me that wanted to play with my friend in the warm water and was disappointed that he didn't want to play with me. The young adult me that had a fantasy honeymoon in mind that didn't fit with my current reality. The wise me that got in touch with how my expectations were contributing to my suffering—suffering that was spilling over onto Larry.

That night I had a transformational dream: it is my wedding day. I am ecstatically happy because I am marrying the man of my dreams. Friends and family along with people I don't know surround me. I look very beautiful in a spectacular white dress. I am so happy because I am marrying Matthew Broderick. I love him so much. He is funny, talented, good, lucky, a delight to be with. I am preparing to enter the church when a woman tells me that I am in trouble: she informs me that Matthew is an axe murderer. If I marry him, he will murder me. I awaken from the dream filled with fear and knowing that someone is about to kill me.

That morning as I walked the beach and reflected on the dream, I realized that Matthew Broderick in the movie *Ferris Bueller's Day Off* was my fantasy lover. In this movie, Ferris is cute, charming, funny, and creative. He can sing, dance, get along with everyone, and work miracles. This was at some level the man that I wanted to marry.

The man I actually married had beard stubble, a bit of a belly, didn't want to play all the time, and was a grump. I realized I had to kill my fantasy or it would kill me. I had to come to terms with my partner as a real human being—a real human being with a full spectrum of emotions. I had to come to terms with my fantasy honeymoon and let that go, too.

Later that day, we were able to talk. I talked about how I had put pressure from unspoken expectations on Larry about marriage and the honeymoon. I apologized and said that although I was disappointed, it was cool. We really did have our whole life.

Larry expressed that he did feel some pressure to be perfectly aligned with my agenda. This seemed to bring out his worst self. We apologized to one another and connected for the first time since the wedding ceremony.

PRACTICE: *Identifying Bones from the Past*		

Set aside some time for quiet reflection and meditation. Enjoy 5–10 minutes of mindful breathing. Have your journal and/or art supplies handy. Some questions for your practice of deep looking:

+ Is there someone from my past that I think of in terms of "if only I had dated or married X?"
+ Is there any other relationship that I compare my relationship to?
+ Is there someone that I find myself comparing my partner to—either a real person or a fantasy person?
+ Do I ever catch myself thinking I am with someone other than my partner?
+ Do I have unfinished business with a former lover, partner, or friend?

SINGING TO SETTLE
THE BONES OF THE PAST

Our broken hearts and broken dreams from the past can haunt us if we don't put them to rest. It's as if we are carrying around bones from the past. Unless we take the time to identify the bones, name them, honor them, release them, and bury them, they can follow us around or add a significant weight to our shoulders. For Larry, it took a while for the skeletons from the past to emerge. Singing was the key to releasing them.

I was married to two fine women before Peggy. While I had shared many values and interests with both of my wives, we had patterns that didn't contribute to our happiness. My first wife and I married right out of high school, and we had a pattern of suppressing our anger and passive aggressive behavior. I didn't want to make this mistake in my second marriage, so we had a pattern of under communicating. I brought both of these patterns into my marriage with Peggy.

Peggy was able to identify and name these ghosts and patterns early on in our relationship. She would say, "I'm not your ex-wife, now go sing!" Still, my initial reaction was to be defensive. I was not in the present moment. I was in my past. Eventually I admitted that even though divorce had been the right decision, I was still carrying the disappointment and heartbreak from these broken dreams.

I love to sing more than I admit. In community college, I was in a singing group that performed way before Mahalia Jackson came on stage. Normally we were engaged to sing for church services. The best services were when we would get cooking on an old hymn and just cut loose, adding verse after verse. A great funeral had at least an hour of singing in this fashion. We were singing to help the spirit to be present. This I experienced in my own being—I could sing to help release ghosts from my past that were preventing me from keeping my appointment with love in the present moment.

I go into a back bedroom, put on the headset, select the music that speaks to me that day, and sing. I generally discover that I have some attachment to my suffering. I find that these bones have some kind of strange beauty. I have fashioned them into something like a pearl and I want to hold on to it. If I keep singing, it feels like I am honoring this strange pearl. It lifts it up so I start to find the peace that is in the space left behind by the bones of my past. This ritual helps me to let go of the suffering. It helps me to recognize that there was something beautiful for me, there was a gift. I can name this, hold it, and then let it go.

THE ENKA

Have you ever been to a Japanese karaoke bar? If so, you know what enka sounds like. We really don't have an equivalent in the West. But we expect many of you are acquainted with karaoke.

Enka is a special type of song created in Japan for mourning a lost love and a broken heart. Most enkas are in a minor key. The songs are sung strongly with a voice full of emotion and a strong, delayed vibrato. They can sound harsh to Western trained ears. The songs are of the sweet resignation about a love that is over or lost. Key themes are songs of endings, desperation, death, break up, and suicide. They are powerfully sweet, tragic, and filled with pathos. They speak to the tragic state of the heart when love is over.

Enka offers an element of ritual and ceremony to the bones of the past and a fantasy love. It attempts to create beauty out of a lost love in a way that captures the event, the person, the place and time, and the love connection. The singing of an enka is an acknowledgment that the love was real, beautiful, it ended tragically, and now it is over. This is not an opportunity to speak unkindly about the former love. It is an opportunity to address the sweet mystery of love and to do so with drama and power.

We both use singing to heal our heartaches. We find music and singing a delightful way to release suffering and return to joy. Larry likes gospel, some musicals and Coltrane. Peggy enjoys hymns, show tunes, Motown, Doo Wop and songs from childhood. We enjoy enka as it introduces drama, beauty, and poetry. And most importantly, it's fun. If we can sing about something, we are en route to being unstuck. It is hard to stay angry, depressed, or confused when we are singing.

> *Irene, good night. Irene, good night.*
> *Good night Irene, good night, Irene. I'll see you in*
> *my dreams."*
> —Classic American version of an enka

PRACTICE: *Create Your Enka for Former Loves*

Select one skeleton or lost love at a time. Write your own song for this love. Or, if there is a song that resonates with you, you can use this song and sing it to this love. Singing the song is an important part of the ritual of honoring and releasing. We give you full permission to sing out loud with drama, flair, pathos, and energy.

CHAPTER NINE

Cold Hells, Hot Hells

❦

When we hold onto the past, we suffer. We react in different ways to this suffering. Larry tends to reside in what Tibetan Buddhist cosmology calls "the cold hells," while Peggy's suffering draws her into the "hot hells". The hot hells are based in our anger, and the cold hells on our indifference. Understanding these metaphorical spaces may help you catch yourself when your love is descending into one of them.

The seven cold hells have landscapes of snow-covered mountains and glaciers perpetually enveloped in blizzards. The beings in these realms are completely naked and unceasingly tormented by the cold. How do you recognize that you're in a cold hell? You may recognize some of these cues:

- Icy language. You're sharp tongued and critical of yourself and others. You may swear to yourself and others and use short sentences with strong punctuation. Your writing becomes terse, your words clipped. Your self-talk and external dialogue may be sarcastic and your tone and terminology negative and defeated.

+ Icy looks. Your eyes get hard, cold. You notice faults, flaws, mistakes, and cracks. You look at the cup as half empty.

+ Icy thoughts. You catch yourself thinking negatively, more globally in terms of bad or good, right or wrong. You might think, "We won't make it," or, "Maybe I'd be better off on my own." "I am not so sure about myself, you, or anyone else." "The world is not a safe place." You may feel that you're getting old.

+ Icy actions. You shut down, turn away, move away from the things that would nourish you and invite happiness. You might read, work, or go online.

Larry's reflection on the cold hells: When my mother first met Peggy, she nodded her head toward me and said: "He just started talking a few years ago." My bedroom in the family home was in the attic. If I wasn't at work or church, I was up in the attic, alone and happy. I would do what Peggy now calls my "Bat cave thing," and put up a wall around whatever feeling arose. It took me several years of mindfulness practice to recognize how this act of self-protection kept me disconnected from myself and from the world.

It's a very lonely thing to be with someone who's not there. When someone is in the cold hell realm, it is the perfect time to offer them the gifts of space and understanding. Offering them your frustration and anger, even your sweetness, at this time will only make that person retreat even further into the cold hells. After a little while has passed, you can check in with them.

PRACTICE: *Personal Reflection on the Cold Hells*

+ What helps you to soften your belly and your heart?
+ What helps you to smooth out your rough edges?
+ What helps you to relax your jaw and your stiff upper lip?
+ What helps you melt?
+ What helps you to remove the icy bricks from the wall, the cold moss, the frozen tundra?

THE HOT HELLS

There are eight hot hells that rest one above the other like the stories of a building. On each story, the floor and walls are like the white-hot iron of a blacksmith. There is nowhere at all where you can put your foot in safety. Everywhere is a searingly hot expanse of fiery flames and blazing heat where tormenters ceaselessly torture you. How do you know you're in hot hells?

+ Hot language. Your speech is emotionally charged and may be loud. You may use unskillful language to express things you've been holding in for a long time. You may swear and blame yourself or others. Your speech and writing may be verbose, unclear, defensive, disorganized. Your self-talk and external dialogue may be angry and self-righteous. You may express things you'll later wish you hadn't said.

+ Hot looks. Your eyes flame. You tend to blame the other person. You may try to communicate with the other, even though you know that without first regaining your calm, you can only make things worse. Or you may shut the other person out and refuse any advances to reconcile because you feel so thoroughly "wronged."

+ Flaming thoughts. Your mind is on fire, your thoughts negative and condemning, and you see things in a dualistic way, in terms of good and bad, right and wrong. You might feel misunderstood or hopeless or as though the world is crazy.

+ Hot actions. Your movements are rushed, uncontrolled; you may inadvertently drop things, knock things down, and bump into things. You may refuse to go outside and walk or do other things you know are nourishing. Instead you'll stay inside, hold onto and prolong your anger, and continue to make those around you suffer.

PRACTICE: *Personal Reflection on the Hot Hells*

Can you identify a firewall? If so, what purpose does it serve. Can you think of a previous firewall that you erected? What helped you to break it down, melt it down, circumvent or dismantle it? What helps you cool down the flames?

When your partner is in the hot or cold hells, remember they are suffering. As long as you are truly physically and emotionally safe from harm, this is the perfect time to give them the gift of no fear, being there with them, even though they try and burn you away or ice you down.

We, Larry and Peggy, recognize that we are baby Buddhas. We continue to practice with deep blocks of old suffering that will rise to the surface in our practice and in our home life. The best medicine for both of us to chase away the heart's burning is to make direct contact with life's sufferings, to touch and share real anxieties and uncertainties with others, to serve others. This breaks down the false sense of separation, the illusion that we are self-contained beings. We can break out of the shell or barrier that we put up to "protect" ourselves from the world. We found that our natural tendency when the old blocks of pain rise up is to want to run away. We now can identify this tendency. We have learned that when we most want to run away, we need to run toward each other or toward our Sangha, our beloved community.

Knives

MATTHEW BORTOLIN

Standing beside the open dishwasher, my eyes narrow with annoyance. "Heather! I asked you to turn these knives down!"

My words are shouted to reach my wife, elevated to pierce through walls and reach unseen ears. Such an effort gives them an unintended edge, sharper than the blades in question. I get no response.

We have a dishwasher in our house but no dishes for it to scrub clean. Not that we are without dinnerware, mind you. We have plenty. Antique, hand-painted stuff full of flowers, swirls, and horse-and-buggy scenes, all gathered from the garages of the deceased, where middle-aged orphans happily take a few dollars for a box of the plates their mother had once served their macaroni and cheese on. Now, without their mother, they have little use for them, ancient and cracked as they are. And, besides, they are not dishwasher safe.

Not dishwasher safe. I feel sorry for our dishwasher, no longer given the opportunity to perform its noble duty.

And that is why the point of the knives is a cause of raised voice. Left open, with the lower rack extended, the retired dishwasher houses a silverware basket bristling with the upturned knives, their edged points jutting at my shins like a crop of medieval caltrops. Should I trip while moving past, could I not find honed steel piercing my bony legs? If I raise a hand to stop the fall, will my palm receive the dreaded Ginsu bite?

'Tis a dangerous trap, I repeatedly tell my wife.

She has a different view on the matter. Downward turned knives, she contends, will dull on the plastic basket and slowly whittle away that silverware sheathe until it can no longer hold even a spatula. Moreover, turned up, the wide steel surface dries quicker and cleaner.

Should the knives point up or down? We can get lost in the debate over these points of view.

In my marriage, it is views that play the role of Iago to my Othello and Heather's Desdemona. Views are ideas we have about the mechanics of life that we formulate based upon our recollections and supposition. Because recollection is rooted in the past and supposition in the future, views can never be about the immediate experience of the present. Life itself, things as they are right now—that's immediate experience. Our views are always a step slow or decades behind.

Views are not life. They are ideas about life that can color and deform what truly is. Views are artificial and bifurcate reality.

Let go of all views, say Buddhist masters. But if truth be told I am quite fond of my views and the act of tossing them aside doesn't come easily.

Views are attractive. They are the ingredients in our stew of identity, the stuff that when mixed together and set to simmer cooks up who we are, what we project to the world. When held for a long time, views become familiar friends, always there to offer comfort. They provide structure and direct choices, actions and words.

I have a view, or perhaps it's more of a motto that is on continual loop in my noggin: *Better to keep silent and be thought a fool than to speak and remove all doubt.* Of course, to hold such a view I must have a foundation of other views to prop it up. The most prominent is the view that I am indeed a great fool and everything I say is naive or as stale as three-week-old bread. So I seal my lips.

I have lived my life hearing about how my older brother is smarter, more charismatic, better looking, a better athlete, and an all around finer human being. Growing up under such a shadow it's easy to attach to a view and motto that cajoles you to keep your fool mouth shut because no matter what you say it'll never be as wise and insightful as your older brother.

Years of competing but falling short leaves one sensitive to criticism and easily stung by those you try so hard to please. Like my wife.

I cross the house to the room where she sits reading.

"Can't we *please* turn the knives down," I ask, this time with less volume.

She snorts and rolls her eyes with mock disgust.

"And ruin my awesome knives? No way, Captain Safety Pants!"

Such a comment, as tame as it is, normally leaves me feeling small and stupid. Eye rolls are especially devastating.

How does one deal with such low self-esteem in the intimate confines of marriage? How do I set aside my prickly pride and take my wife's comments with good humor? How do I stop feeling like a second rate little brother and start standing tall like a worthy human being?

I know of no perfect formula that I can apply to one state of mind in order to transform into another, more likeable one. Contemplations and visualizations might prove beneficial to some, but to me they are dangerous. Willing myself to adopt an ideal or become an aggrandized, even cherished model, like a confident person or a Buddha, is missing the mark.

That day with the knives and Heather's gibe, I discovered that pride, self-doubt, and my abysmal self-esteem weren't there. They just didn't surface. I never tried to get rid of them, so where did my constant companions go? Why didn't I turn nasty at Heather's verbal poke? How did I rid myself of those unwanted views?

As I have practiced, I've found that reactions just don't arise with the frequency and force that they once did. I did not will this to happen, it just did, to my continuous amazement. The practice I am referring to is meditation. Just sitting.

It's just like with the knives. Up or down doesn't quite say it. One point of view is not truer than another. Those knives, they're just reality. But even that's not quite right because "reality" is just another concept. The knives, the dishwasher, me and my concepts, even me here now writing about that memory, trying my best to express myself clearly and sound wise—it's all just what is. And there's nothing wrong or right about any of it.

To accept things as they are is the practice of Buddhism. So, does it matter which direction the knives point? I grin wryly at my wife, tip my cap at her jest, and return to the dishwasher, perfectly accepting the upward pointing knives. Then I turn each of them down. Just in case.

HABIT ENERGIES

In a relationship, each partner can get into the habit of going into the cold or the hot hells instead of being present with their loved one. We're also in the habit of running away from our suffering and thinking that happiness lies only in the future. If we practice mindfulness, then whenever the energy of wanting to run away arises, we can smile at it and say, "Hello, my old friend, I recognize you." We practice so that our happiness is present here and now. Life and happiness are to be found only in the present moment. Many habit energies are seeds handed down to us through our parents and many generations of ancestors. Even if we're determined to do the opposite of what our parents did, unless we know how to practice and transform these seeds, we'll do just as they did.

Habit energy is an important term in Buddhist psychology. The seeds we receive from our ancestors, friends, society, and the environment are held in our consciousness. It's only when these seeds manifest in our mind consciousness that we become aware of them. There may be times we think there's no seed of anger in us. However, as soon as someone irritates us, our seed of anger makes itself known. Our habit energies affect the way we see, feel, and behave; they keep us from perceiving things as they truly are. But it's possible for us to change our habit energies. In fact, in order to transform ourselves we must change them. Even if we have the best intention to transform, we won't be successful unless we work on our habit energies.

Through the practice of mindfulness, we can identify the seeds in ourselves and recognize the habit energies that go along with them. With mindfulness, we can observe our habit energies and begin to transform them. The practice of mindfulness allows us to create new, beneficial habits. When we hear something that displeases us, instead of going to the hot or cold hells, we can go back to our breathing. It doesn't come naturally at first, but if we continue to practice, instead of pushing our partner away or firing hurtful words when we're angry, we can establish the habit of conscious breathing. We can let our anger arise and let it go without needing to hold on tight.

PRACTICE: *Meditation for When I'm Angry at My Partner*

Very often those with whom we get most angry are those we most love. Our anger is a function of that deep love, which can be released by this exercise. You can practice this in a meditation time, or you can practice it "on the spot". You will see very quickly that life is precious, time is short! No need to squander your great love.

Aware of my body alive and breathing, I breathe in.
Smiling to my body alive and breathing, I breathe out.

Seeing my body 100 years in the future, I breathe in.
Smiling to my body 100 years in the future, I breathe out.

Aware of my beloved 100 years in the future, I breathe in.
Smiling to my beloved 100 years in the future, I breathe out.

Seeing the dead body of my beloved lying in bed, I breathe in.
Smiling to the dead body of my beloved, I breathe out.

Seeing my beloved and myself in three hundred years, I breathe in.
Seeing my beloved and myself in three hundred years, I breathe out.

Will You Breathe
With Me, My Dear

SUSAN GLOGOVAC

Two months into a home remodel, our patience was wearing thin. Our daily routine had been disrupted. We were living in a much smaller space, sharing in ways that were new and exciting but that also tested our ability to live in peace and harmony in the midst of a constant flow of workers coming in and out, a significant amount of dirt and dust, and so many decisions to be made.

One day, we were standing together in the middle of the remodel space, trying to make yet another decision—a pretty small one relative to all those we had been making—about finishing a doorway. Neither of us was particularly enthusiastic about making this decision, yet as we talked about possibilities, we found ourselves getting attached to the option we were offering.

This felt all too familiar, a pathway we have walked many times during the thirty-plus years we have lived together. And I think we both knew that no good would come from walking this path of widening differences that at first were so small.

Still, our habit energies were strong and we moved ahead, getting more and more impatient with each other and ourselves.

In the midst of this growing misery, I was able to connect with myself. I noticed how unhappy I was becoming. Still, I didn't know how to change direction, to move us out of this place of suffering. So I paused and asked for help from my partner. I said, "I need your help right now. Would you be willing to hold my hands and breathe with me?"

My dear husband reached out to help me, to help us. He enfolded my hands in his. We stood in the middle of the room and closed our eyes, breathing together.

Slowing, our breathing eased and merged into one breath. The energy coursing through us changed from irritation and frustration to deep peacefulness.

When we opened our eyes, we smiled to each other and shared a hug. In the midst of those breaths, what seemed like a large problem dissolved into what it had been all along: an issue to address and solve collaboratively. There was nothing else that needed to be said or done. So simple and deeply profound to practice, to be able to stop and breathe together, in order to calm ourselves and return to our center of peace and love. With those shared breaths, we were able to touch our true nature, our Buddha nature, and to come home to ourselves and to each other.

CHAPTER TEN

Healing and Transformation

You are always being asked to heal yourself. To know the pain, rage and grief you carry in your own heart enables you to take your place on the path of all healing.

—Christina Feldman, from *Compassion*

We are inspired by Christina Feldman's insight. When we accept this invitation to come home to ourselves, we touch our deep humanity. In the practice of healing and transforming, we are restored to our unique partnership and our love energy.

The spiritual space you and your partner have created in your own hearts is the best place to go when you are having difficulty. Here we use the practice of breathing, the insight of compassionate understanding, skills of artful listening, and loving speech.

THE MEDICINE OF UNDERSTANDING

Be not disturbed at being misunderstood
Be disturbed rather at not understanding.
—Chinese Proverb

It is very human to want to be understood, especially by our partner. One of the most powerful gifts we can give our beloved one is the balm of understanding. In Mahayana Buddhism, perfect understanding is described as the mother of all Buddhas. Everything that is awake, compassionate, and beautiful is born from her.

It's important to recognize that understanding doesn't necessarily mean agreeing with one another: it means acceptance. This is a common stumbling block for couples. It is human nature to believe that if our partner truly understood, then he or she would agree with us. Going over and over these areas of "misunderstanding" in search of agreement is a common pattern in relationships. Some people take communication classes on verbal expression and get more and more skillful at expressing their own truth, but they may still be seeking agreement rather than understanding.

Our understanding and acceptance of our partner is a direct and immediate experience of how we're understanding and accepting ourselves. When working with large groups, we sometimes ask everyone to get up off their folding chairs and lie the chairs down. Next, we ask people to talk their chairs into coming upright. They can say whatever they want but can't physically move the chairs.

Some people talk to their chairs quietly. Others go on their knees pleading, others point fingers. Some yell at the chair: "Get with it! Be a chair." The exercise may seem silly, but it can be an effective reminder of the futility of trying to talk someone into changing. It doesn't matter if you cry, beg, or yell, you can't force another person (or a chair) to change.

We often believe that if we speak or act differently, our partner will change. Instead, if we can learn to listen deeply to our partner in order to hear and understand who they truly are, and if we can respond to them with loving speech, transformation will occur naturally.

If we can learn to listen deeply to our partner in order to hear and understand who they truly are at this moment, we give the flower of compassion a chance to be born in our heart. If we can respond to them with loving speech, kind presence, and a smile, healing and transformation can occur naturally.

PRACTICE: *Understanding Myself*

+ Set aside some time for quiet reflection. Have your journal, pen and/or art supplies handy. Center yourself and enjoy 5–10 minutes of breathing.
+ Read or recite the following phrase as a self-blessing: "May I learn to look at myself with the eyes of understanding and love." Recite this blessing and continue to enjoy your breath. When thoughts arise, repeat the phrase. (*5 minutes*)
+ Choose one specific situation or aspect of yourself

that you would like to better understand. Name this topic, situation, or aspect of yourself and return to your breathing. Bring the light of mindfulness and concentration into your meditation. As your thoughts drift of from the object of your concentration, gently bring your mind back by repeating your topic. (*5–10 minutes*)

+ Close your practice time with the self blessing: "May I learn to look at myself with the eyes of understanding and love."

+ Journal or draw about your experience of this practice of self understanding. How might you share with your partner what you are discovering about yourself?

The Medicine of Understanding

CO LAN

After thirty years of marriage, I am so glad that my husband finally understands what I am saying. It took him thirty years, and now he wants to know what I am thinking. Oh my goodness! It might take him another thirty years for that, and I don't know if I will still be here for him to understand. But to understand a person, between a husband and wife, it is not so easy. This is partly because I don't want to say things all the time. I want him to guess. And if he doesn't guess right, he doesn't want to do exactly what I want and I become upset with him.

He says to me, "Why don't you tell me what you want?" And I say, "I don't want to have to tell you all the time." Then he says, "How do I know?" And I say, "Well, we've been living here for a long time together and you should know."

Sometimes my husband is absent-minded and he doesn't remember things. And I have this tendency to remember a lot of things, lots of little things. But I am getting better at not expecting him to understand and remember like I do. I have learned that if I expect him to do things without me telling him, that I will suffer. And I have this tendency to make him suffer, too.

127

A few weeks ago, my husband came to me and asked if I wanted to go to Deer Park, a Buddhist retreat center in Southern California, on Saturday. He didn't say, "I really want to go to Deer Park." He asked me if I would like to go to Deer Park. I knew that meant that he wanted to go, so I arranged everything. Because I understood that arranging to go to Deer Park would make him happy. And his happiness makes me happy. This is what is making our relationship work. We understand that if you make your partner happy, than you are happy. It works every time.

PRACTICE: *Deep Listening*

There are two key techniques to understanding yourself and your partner—deep looking (discussed in Chapter Two) and deep listening. Psychotherapists often try to practice deep listening, to sit quietly and listen to you with a lot of compassion—not in order to judge, criticize, condemn, or evaluate, but with a single purpose: helping you to suffer less. If someone can listen to you like that for one hour, you feel much better. Anyone who wants to listen deeply needs to practice maintaining compassion and concentration while listening. Anyone who wants to listen deeply needs to practice maintaining compassion and attention while listening.

Practice breathing mindfully in and out and remind yourself, "I'm listening to him or to her not to know what's inside of that person or offer advice. I'm listening because I want to relieve their suffering."

Sometimes while listening, irritation or anger may arise, making it difficult to continue to listen. If halfway through listening, irritation or anger comes up, it won't be possible to continue to listen. So you have to practice in a way that whenever this energy comes up, you can breathe in and out mindfully and continue to hold compassion. No matter what the other person says, even if the person speaks with strong emotion, even if what they says contains misperceptions and an unjust view, if we can listen like this to our beloved ones, they will feel much better

If you don't feel that you can continue to listen in this way, ask your partner, "Dear one, can we continue in a few days? I need to renew myself. It is my desire to listen to you in the best way I can." If we feel we haven't listened well enough, we can promise to do better next time we have a chance to practice deep listening.

LOVING SPEECH

If we can learn to listen genuinely, profoundly, and lovingly, we create a loving environment of deep safety and caring. However, many of us have lost our ability to listen and to use loving speech. In many relationships communication has become almost impossible. In part, this is because of the busyness of our lives and our confusion with the means of communication. We have many innovative ways that we can communicate—email, cell phones, text messages—and yet the quality of our communication is lacking in depth and skill. Thich Nhat Hanh shares the following mantras for couples. A mantra is a phrase that has the power to transform the situation. The first mantra is, "I am here for you." Just these few simple words are a deep practice in being whole-heartedly present for your partner.

The second mantra is, "I know you are there, my dear, and it makes me very happy." This mantra nourishes wholesome seeds of happiness and joy. In saying this mantra, it is important to feel the meaning of these words. You are saying, "I know you are here with me, alive on the planet. This alone is a miracle, and I am truly grateful for the gift of your presence in my life."

The Gift of Gatha

ALEXA SINGER-TELLES

While meditating on the sultry shores of the Puget Sound, we were invited to participate in a simple gatha writing exercise. A gatha is a short phrase used to increase one's mindfulness when engaged in an activity. The first line of the poem was to name a challenging situation in our lives. I wrote something that happened frequently in my marriage: "In the midst of an argument with my partner …" We then passed the paper to our left, and that person was invited to add the next phrase. She added, "I vow with all beings …" The paper was then passed to a third person who called on their inner wisdom to write a final line that would offer some practical, mindful response to the dilemma. The final line that came back to me read: "… to still my immediate reactions and to look deeply into my partner's heart." This seemed like good advice.

The gatha written on that scrap of paper has been in my dresser for years. I've picked it up and reread it many times. It's helped me prevent an argument from escalating, calm myself, and have the composure and compassion to look deeply into my husband's suffering. When I realize that we are both react-ing angrily from hurt, miscommunication, or old family wounds and patterns, I'm able to stop our war by letting go of my attachment to my position and connecting with the love I have for my husband. I remember my commitment to nonviolent communication and a peaceful relationship. When I can voice my concerns calmly and apologize for my part in our skirmish, my husband can breathe and reflect on his own heart. He, too, has learned the power of an apology. His ability to take time and return to me with increased awareness and responsibility for his mistakes has deepened my respect and love for him.

The third mantra is, "I know you are suffering. That is why I am here for you." Sitting close to them, being present, and saying this mantra, can in itself bring them a lot of relief. If you're not certain how the other person is feeling, or if these words seem too direct for the situation, you can say something like, "Is everything okay?" or "Is something the matter?"

The fourth mantra is to ask for help from your partner when you are suffering. The mantra is, "I am suffering. Please help." This can be the most difficult mantra to use. These are vulnerable words. It may take a long time of personal mindfulness practice before you are comfortable saying them. You're saying that you're experiencing pain and you're asking for help from your partner. It is precisely because you're modeling no fear and exposing your vulnerability that this mantra is so powerful.

We often use letter writing for the purpose of expressing our deep commitment to our partnership, our appreciations and joy, as well as hurt and difficulty. Sometimes, along with the letter, we place a rose in our vase, as described in Chapter Five. We have an agreement that we sit with the letter, without discussing it, for two or three days. We recommend you try this as opposed to talking right away. This gives both of you time to reflect. At the end of a few days, see if your partner wants to talk. If so, make a date to talk about the letter. When we were first married, there were a lot more letters on our altar. Now, we're better able to integrate loving speech and deep listening into our everyday activities.

PRACTICE: *Writing a Love Letter*

Settle down into a quite space with pen and paper. Practice 5-10 minutes of mindful breathing. Set your intention to write a letter to your beloved using loving speech, while you write the letter, practice looking openly into the nature of your relationship. Writing a letter is an authentic form of meditation. Ask yourself: What do you appreciate about your love? What do you wish to celebrate? What seeds and qualities do you want to water? Peace, understanding, and compassion have transformed you.

Your letter can express your love and also acknowledge your mistakes—the times you have spoken or acted unskillfully with your beloved. We do not talk in terms of right or wrong, good or evil, but as "more skillful" and "less skillful," "more mindful" and "less mindful." This makes the situation lighter, "I was unmindful. I was not mindful enough" instead of "I was wrong, you were right," or "You were wrong, I was right." "I was not skillful. I am sorry."

You may begin your letter, "It's funny, I have learned so much from my unskillfulness and suffering. Through these I have been able to grow. I want to share with you what I have discovered." Writing the letter can bring you insight. You look into yourself, bring the past into the present, and practice looking deeply into the past. You do not lose yourself in the past at all; you are still grounded in the present moment. The object of your study is your relationship with your beloved. When you examine your relationship, try to be honest and sincere. You want to be fully present, fully alive. That is why your letter is a process of discovery and a declaration of love.

BEGINNING ANEW

> *Ring the bell that still can ring, forget your perfect offering. There is a crack in everything. That's how the light gets in.*
>
> —Leonard Cohen

We have a practice called Beginning Anew that's part of Thich Nhat Hanh's tradition. It's an opportunity for people who live together, whether as a couple, a family, or a community, to come together and practice deep listening and loving speech. Its intention is to set in motion a fresh start in a relationship.

It is comprised of three skills: flower watering, expressing regrets, and expressing hurts and difficulties. These skills can play an important role in transforming the deepest parts of our consciousness and our love to begin anew. They provide an opportunity to deepen our shared understanding and initiate our shared healing. They are a protection and a guide to finding a way back to a loving relationship with our partner, and in the process they transform our hearts and minds.

This practice can be done in a set aside space at a regular time as it is offered in the Plum Village community. For a couple and family, we have discovered many ways to make Beginning Anew a part of our daily life.

FLOWER WATERING

Flower watering is the foundation skill of Beginning Anew. It is an exchange of appreciation between you and your partner. To begin, choose an appropriate location or space. It's nice to have a flower in a vase near you. Enjoy 10–15 minutes of mindful breathing to calm yourself.

When you're ready to speak, pick up the flower or the vase. Look at the flower in front of you and then at the flower that is your partner. This is an opportunity for us to express appreciation, validation, and acknowledgment of our partner. Seek only the positive seeds that you want to water in your partner and in your relationship: seeds of compassion, joy, equanimity, humor, patience, and diligence. Only one person at a time speaks. When you've finished speaking, return the flower to its place, and then your partner can have a turn.

The skill of flower watering can be expressed in other times and places. This might be a walk in the park, on the beach, or at a favorite restaurant or coffee shop. Our affirmation of our partnership can also be expressed through cards, notes, poems, songs, or a smile.

When we lived in a community, we did flower watering every Wednesday night. Every other week the children joined us. We sat together in a circle and enjoyed this time very much. We all grew more adept at watering the seeds that were sprouting and the flowers already in bloom, and it helped to build a stable and happy community life.

We discovered that if we had a deep practice of flower watering, our regrets and disappointments could be healed right away. We often don't need to move on to the next practice. We recommend that you do just flower watering for a few weeks and strengthen this practice before moving to the second part of Beginning Anew.

EXPRESSING REGRET

We've grown in solidity through the practice of mindfulness and the skill of flower watering. It is easier to speak from the heart from this place of solidity and freedom. The second skill of Beginning Anew is to mindfully express any regrets. Flower watering must occur before the expression of regret. Reflect on the past few weeks and see if there's something you've done or said that you regret.

Express regret for anything you've done to hurt your partner. Only the person holding the flower speaks. Use loving speech to name the situation as clearly as you can. Your partner's only work is to practice breathing and deep listening, not blaming, arguing, or even agreeing. When you've finished, put the flower in the middle for your partner's turn.

EXPRESSING HURT AND DIFFICULTY

The third skill is the mindful expression of hurt and difficulty. You only need to do this practice when it is necessary and appropriate.

Again, one person speaks at a time holding the flower. The other person listens and doesn't interrupt. Even if you hear something that you believe isn't true, sit, breathe, and listen. Just by listening patiently, you can alleviate a great deal of pain and suffering in your beloved one. Both parties seek to identify how they have contributed to the situation. See if you can find yourself in this story. You can close your time together by holding hands, taking a walk, having a cup of tea. You are done with the discussion and you enjoy each other's company.

A NEW YEAR

The New Year is a special opportunity to Begin Anew. Set aside some quiet time for reflection, contemplation, and companionship. It would be great if you could schedule a retreat with your partner. Or, perhaps an urban retreat: with two hours on Saturday and two hours on Sunday. Prepare the space so that you have the food and supplies that you need. Set the ground rules for your time together: some of our ground rules: we won't answer the phone, watch TV, or get on the computer. We try to not use our car.

PRACTICE: *The New Year Collage*

◆ Prepare yourselves and your space for a retreat. Have art supplies that include magazines, glue sticks, scissors, and poster board handy. Then introduce to your meditation practice the following questions: What are my hopes and dreams for this New Year—for myself as an individual, for my partner and myself, for my relationship to my work and family, and for myself as a steward of the planet? What would I like to experience this year? What do I want to learn this year? How do I want to live my life this year? What

Beginning Anew

BARBARA CASEY

My husband and I celebrated our twenty-first anniversary this week. Growing our relationship has been the most challenging thing I've ever done, and it is the greatest treasure in my life.

For years, I have been stubborn and egotistical, stuck on the sureness of my point of view. Somehow, slowly, our edges have softened, and we are now able to hold different views without threatening the other. It has become more important that we are both happy than that either of us gets our way.

I remember so many occasions, often in the kitchen preparing dinner at the end of a busy day; one of us would bring up a difficult subject, usually around money or work. And it would inevitably end badly. Then we learned about the practice of Beginning Anew. Now we use this practice not only to mend but also as a process of kind communication. We have also learned to do this practice informally, sometimes in public without others even knowing what we are doing. When tension rises, we have learned to drop our story line, take some deep breaths, look each other in the eye, and say, "I don't want to be mad at you." Learning to let go quickly has relieved us of so much suffering.

Here's what I want to say to my partner and to you. Every moment of this relationship, from the worst to the most transcendent, has been a gift. As often happens, some of the best times have been disguised in difficulty. I remember several times when my unskillful expressions of my deepest fears came to the surface, and I realized later that it could only have happened in the container of love and safety my husband provided. To have someone encouraging me gently to be my best and holding me in loving acceptance when I fall short is the greatest happiness.

seeds do I want to water in my soul garden, relationship garden, and in the world's garden? What do I
want to weed out this year? What do I want to cultivate? What do I want to harvest? Where do I want
to place my fertilizer?

+ After 15–20 minutes of reflection, it is time to slowly
and mindfully leaf through the magazines. Keep
repeating the questions to connect to yourself, your
partner, and the world. Cut out the images that call
you, grab your attention, capture you. After about
20 minutes of collecting the images, stop gathering.
Come back to your poster board. Sometimes I like
to make a large circle, a mandala, to begin. With a
gentle focus on the questions about yourself, your
partner and the world, create your collage.

+ When your collages are ready, sit with them for a
while. Let them breathe and then speak to you. What
do you hear? What do you notice? What stands out?
Share your collage and your insights with your partner. One person speaks at a time.

+ After listening to each other, please bow and offer a
blessing to your partner for the New Year. Then it's
a good idea to get practical. This might be in another
block of time, but it is critical that you get your calen-
dars out and work out some of the ideas. Put them on
the calendar. Take things off the calendar. Re-invent
your lives and Begin Anew.

FORGIVENESS

> Genuine forgiveness is participation, reunion overcoming the powers of estrangement. We cannot love unless we have accepted forgiveness, and the deeper our experience of forgiveness is, the greater is our love."
>
> —Paul Tillich

Forgiveness is the experience of finding peace in ourselves. It cannot be willed, and it cannot be obstructed by another. Our wholehearted participation in the process of healing and transforming creates the space where forgiveness can occur.

Forgiveness does not mean that we condone a harmful action, or that we are denying or repressing injustice or suffering. It shouldn't be confused with being silent or passive in the face of violence or abuse. If you're suffering physical or emotional abuse, immediately leave the place where that's going on. Some of us find it particularly hard to forgive ourselves. We're human beings. We're going to make mistakes. We're going to hurt others. Sometimes we do this deliberately, but often we harm others without intending to. This causes us great suffering and can cause us to withdraw from others and disengage from life. When we can forgive another and ourselves, we find ourselves in a place of grace and healing.

When you forgive, you do it for yourself. It will not work to think that you are forgiving for the sake of another being. You have to do it for yourself—completely, energetically, and passionately for your own well being. Then it is full possible that forgiveness will occur.

PRACTICE: *Forgiveness Meditation*

1. Settle into your place of rest and reflection. Put your attention on your breath and calm your body and mind (5–10 *minutes*).

2. Recall the energy of goodness and loving kindness. Say the words "goodness" and "loving kindness" and recall the energy of love that you have given and received. Breathe in, radiating the light of forgiveness toward your heart. Experience your deep friendship and acceptance of yourself.

3. Invite the energy of forgiveness into your heart for anything you feel you've done wrong. Forgive yourself for past errors, commissions, and omissions. They're long gone. Understand that you're a different person and that the person you are today in this moment is forgiving you the errors of your past. Feel the energy of forgiveness filling you and enveloping you with a sense of peace. Feel the light, warmth, and vibration of forgiveness.

4. Think of the people that you hold nearest and dearest. Forgive them for anything you think they've done wrong. Imagine that you're extending the light of forgiveness and radiating this light to them. Let them feel loving kindness, acceptance, tolerance, peace.

5. Now invite your friends to be present in your awareness. Forgive them for anything that you have disliked them for. Imagine whatever has bothered you about them and let that go. Give them the gift of acceptance; let them be their own selves. Imagine embracing them with the energy of love and forgiveness.

6. Invite your parents to be present. Forgive them for anything they've done wrong, for anything you have blamed them for. Understand that they, too, are different today than they were then. Let this forgiveness extend from your heart to them, surrounding them with the radiant light of loving kindness.

7. Think of the people you know, whoever they might be, and forgive them for whatever it is that you have judged, blamed, or disliked them for. Extend your love and forgiveness like a mantle, a blanket of light and love, giving them space and acceptance to be as they are.

8. Invite a person whom you really would like to forgive, someone for whom you are harboring dislike, resentment, and rejection. Forgive him or her fully. Everyone has suffering. Let this forgiveness extend from your heart to theirs. Reach out from your heart and accept them one-hundred percent the way they are. Say to them, "I forgive you and I release any negativity I have held toward you."

9. Think of any person, situation, or group of people whom you have been condemning, blaming, judg-

ing, or actively disliking. Imagine them in front of you and offer your light of forgiveness, extending your regret and your resolve to be deeply at peace with them. Offer your love.

10. Take a look and see if there is anyone or anything else for which you are harboring resentment. Take this opportunity to forgive, extending radiant warmth and light.

11. Bring your attention back to your own heart. Recognize the goodness of your own heart and intention to forgive. Recognize that forgiveness is a process and accept the efforts you're making in the direction of loving kindness. Feel the warmth and ease of forgiveness in your own heart.

12. Complete the meditation practice by extending the merit of the practice to all beings. May all beings have forgiveness in their hearts.

PART THREE

Loving All Beings

CHAPTER ELEVEN

Befriending the World

The Dharma is found in this world and not in another. To leave this world to search for the Dharma is as futile as searching for a rabbit with horns.

—Hui Neng, 6th patriarch of Chan, 618–713 c.e.

As we develop loving kindness for our partner and ourselves, the equanimity, compassion, sympathetic joy, and generosity that blossom will naturally begin to extend beyond our partner relationship. When our vision and practice are not solely focused on one another, our love can continue to grow to include others and our relationships will flourish.

Teilhard de Chardin, the French scientist and philosopher, wrote that conscious love grows out in a wide arc to include the universe and a kinship with all of life. He describes it as "love of the universe [that] develops in boundless light and power." The Dagara people of Burkina Faso believe that when two people live a spirited and balanced intimate life, they have the power to heal everything around them. The Buddha taught his students to enlarge their capacity to love so that their hearts and minds become like a clear flowing river that can accept everything without being contaminated. Any experience—good, bad, or neutral—can be tossed in and purified by the river. Thanks to the power of loving kindness that radiates from our heart and mind, we won't be harmed.

Love grows in ever-widening circles. This begins on our meditation cushion when we make friends with ourselves. Then this love and friendship extends out to one other person. We don't need to be with a partner to experience this widening arc of love; the other person can be our parent, child, sibling, teacher, or friend.

THE NEUTRAL PERSON

The practice of loving kindness begins with extending loving kindness toward ourselves, as in the loving kindness practices discussed in the section on loving yourself. We then build on this energy by remembering benefactors and others we find easy to love. This helps our hearts to soften and expand. Next, we can call a neutral person to mind.

At first it might seem difficult to find someone we would describe as neutral. We may find that we're very quick to have an opinion about everyone. This is normal; our mind is very quick to put people into categories of "like" or "dislike." We can train ourselves to practice loving kindness for someone we may have overlooked or ignored. Our heart and mind have to practice how not to be indifferent or stingy with our love, but how to extend it to a stranger. It may be helpful to start with someone that you don't know well. This might be a person who lives down the road, a clerk at the grocery store, or a person in line at the post office.

If we practice first on someone we like, then on someone neutral to us, then on someone we love, we can then try the most challenging loving kindness meditation, practicing on someone who makes us suffer. Truly wishing love and happiness to someone who has done you harm requires a lot of practice, but it can also be immensely satisfying. Once you're able to do this, the love you have for yourself and for those close to you can expand exponentially.

PRACTICE: *The Neutral Person*

1. Settle into your place of stability and freedom. Practice mindful breathing for 5–10 minutes, coming home to yourself.

2. Recall memories and the energy of goodness. Breathe into the memories and energy of goodness and your own aspiration for love and happiness.

3. Read or recall the loving kindness blessing: "May I be free from danger. May I have mental happiness. May I have physical happiness. May I have ease of well-being." Gently repeat the phrase and rest with the feelings and sensation of this self-blessing. See this prayer as a radiant energy of light and love.

4. Now welcome a teacher or a beloved friend. Imagine that person there with you in your sacred space. Extend the loving kindness prayer to this person. "May you be free from danger. May you have mental happiness. May you have physical happiness. May you have ease of well-being."

5. See if you can bring to mind a neutral person, someone about whom you have no feeling of good or bad, right or wrong. It can be helpful to imagine someone that you just noticed in passing—at the gas station, grocery store, in an elevator. It also might be challenging to try to find someone about whom you didn't have an instant judgment. This is how our mind and brain works. Our mind very quickly likes to sort things out and categorize. It is trying to be helpful.

6. Bring the neutral person to mind or imagine that person in front of you. This is someone who wants to be healthy and happy just as we do. Extend the loving kindness blessing to this person.

7. Thank the neutral person for their help. Close the practice by extending loving kindness and offering the merit from your practice to all beings. Then take a few moments to reflect. What did you learn about yourself with the practice of the neutral person?

There are variations on this loving kindness meditation that exist in many other traditions. There's a traditional Navajo practice called the Beauty Way Blessing. As a daily practice, you extend your awareness of the beauty and blessings that lie in all directions. The words are: "Beauty is above me, beauty below me, beauty to my right, beauty to my left, beauty before me, beauty behind me, beauty all through me, and beauty all around me. I live in beauty, I walk in beauty, and I am in beauty." Sometimes pollen is used to trace a circle around the practitioner.

In Christian mystical tradition, there's a practice of walking to a quiet place in nature for contemplation and prayer. The person takes a rope and makes a circle around him, placing himself in the center. He then extends prayers and blessings in all directions.

The key to loving kindness practice is to visualize the world and the people in it in all their various forms and to wish them well. This practice can be done daily, weekly, or in the moment, wherever we happen to find ourselves.

To befriend our partner, the world, and ourselves we focus on developing loving kindness by recalling and experiencing the goodness within ourselves and others. To see the goodness, we must acknowledge what is difficult while holding our focus on what is positive, true, and beautiful. This takes some practice!

Four Days Ago

KIN HSIEH

Four days ago, two friends and I bought drinks and ice cream at the little corner grocery. Happy with our treasures, we paid the nice lady at the register, smiling and thanking her as we left.

Today, the nice lady is dead. She died the next day. The police report said "it was determined that the death was not natural and that the victim had suffered a fatal gunshot wound." The paramedics found her on the floor, behind the register.

I feel as if I've been struck. And almost in the next instant, something more disturbing: the brushstrokes of a kind of urban stoicism arise, retouching my emotions: "Actually, this happens all the time"; "You didn't really know her, anyway"; "Stuff like that's just part of living in the city"; "Life goes on."

Another part of my mind rises up and disagrees, vehemently. That's denying reality, it shouts, not staying present with it. The reality is that a unique human being has lost her life, and this world is poorer for it. The reality is that this human being touched others' lives, and her customers, friends and family suffer. The reality is that somewhere there is someone who committed an act of aggression, and the weight of this act means they will suffer, too. The reality is that the aggressor's actions touch others known to them, and this also has its consequences. The seeds of fear, anger, and hatred have been sown.

What does it mean to practice mindfulness right now? The question arises, and takes hold. It anchors me.

"Stay present with your emotions," a quiet voice instructs. Dropping my attention down into the body, I close my eyes. I feel heavy, weight pulling on my neck and shoulders. Relaxing on an out-breath, my shoulders drop with a shuddering sigh. A kind of energy vibrates in my arms and torso, radiating down and exiting through tingling fingertips. Moving upward, I feel as though I've swallowed a stone. As I focus on that stone it dissolves, releasing a wave of grief that bubbles up from a well deep inside me and spills down my cheeks.

I sit in front of my computer, feeling the expansion of my abdomen and rib cage as I breathe in, following the contraction as I breathe out. In, out. In, out.

After a while, I begin to see things. I see that the vibration in my hands, arms and chest is the nervous energy of anger, outraged at injustice in this world and itching to do something, to make the perpetrator pay. I see also contained in that is the energy of fear, of being reminded yet again that we may have less control over life than we think, that our safety and security may be less sacrosanct than we think. I see once more that retribution cannot be the way, because it only shifts the burden from one person to another, and I see that until I took the time to pay attention to my experience, I was anxious and irritable with others, thereby unwittingly passing on my own fear and anger in a hundred small ways.

I light a small candle for the slain woman in the little grocery store. Studying the golden flame, I offer a wordless prayer for peace in honor of her life.

I want to live in a world where the suffering of others is not just an anonymous blurb in the police blotter, but a reminder of our fragile and common humanity. I want to live in a world where everyone takes the time to feel the sorrow of tragedies we encounter, to transform the seeds of fear and anger that they sow, so that we do not unwittingly allow them to sprout somewhere else, but use their energy to continue to bless life. Think of the implications of that. There would be no time for wars.

I want to live in a world where each instance of suffering is taken as an opportunity to practice true compassion and to rededicate ourselves to peace, and so I try to practice as if I do.

PRACTICE: *Write a Love Letter to the World*

Bring your writing and art supplies into your meditation space. Enjoy breathing for 15–20 minutes of calming and settling. Invite your loving attention to touch your heart, to breathe into your wellspring of deep aspirations.

Then invite into your meditation some deep and brave questions. Here are some examples: What are my hopes and dreams for the world? And in particular, what are my hopes and dreams connected to my actions in the world? What are my deepest dreams, wildest wishes, and highest hopes for myself, my community, and my planet? What is calling me into greatness? What is tugging at me to live larger? How can I be kinder, gentler, more useful to my journey? And how can we help make this happen? How can I and my beloved engage this in a supportive, nourishing, and delightful way? What is calling us?

Sit with these questions for whatever length of time feels comfortable. Then when you are ready, give yourself at least an hour to write your letters, explore your poems, compost your songs, or craft your art. When you and your partner are done, read your letters aloud. Read them slowly. Just listen to each other's stories. Do not respond at this time. Just hold your partner's prayers for the world. Bow to each other when you have listened to the love letters and explored the craft. Set a most important date when you can talk about these dreams, but for now, let them settle. Take a walk, go on a hike, or dance. But please, do something together that has physical movement.

Larry's Love Letter to the World

LARRY WARD

I have been hurt by falling dreams
tumbling down like great stones from
the mountain of hope, cracking
open my heart.

I have had the feeling of losing everything
the sound of being ground up by
the world of endurance
tired, sad, and weary
my heart overflowing with tears.

I have met my own fury, coursing
through my veins
as a silent illness
because life did not go my way.

I even thought the moon stole my shoes.
I searched everywhere,
over the green countryside
the crowded city streets,
the brown deserts, the snow-capped mountains,
and even the dust of stars.

I found myself wrapped in
clouds of doubt.
In the softness
of one holy night
the Dharma rain fell.
The sky cleared.
I looked down
and discovered that my shoes
had been on my feet
all along.

My pure heart and my pure mind
have not been crushed or destroyed
by this world's experiences of
disappointment and hatred,
violence and discrimination.

My deepest desire
at this moment
is to be a poem
and live a prayer
that encourages more love
in this world.

It is possible to misperceive the mindfulness teachings and practices handed down over centuries, as if they are solely focused on individual improvement and enlightenment. Certainly, individual improvement and enlightenment are very important. Thich Nhat Han has often said, "Enlightenment is not an individual matter." In fact it is a very important collective matter. The mindfulness tradition calls us home to our true hearts and minds, to the realization of our true identity and our connectedness to all of life with history in the present moment and to recognize how our thinking, speech, and action can effect our time and generations to come.

The love meditations and practices we have offered are designed to train our hearts and minds to access motivations beyond the driving influences of consumerism and preoccupation with self-comfort. Mindfulness of love asks us to acknowledge not only our fractured lives but our broken societies as well. This acknowledgment is done with the humility and power of compassion. With the eyes of the mind of love, one can see that we live in a most remarkable time in human history. Breakthroughs in technology, medicine, science, literacy, democracy, ecology, planetary consciousness, and human well-being have advanced. With these same eyes of love one can see that our previous social-spiritual contract between family, community, tribes, nations, peoples, and nature has run its course. The courage and wisdom to invent a new social-spiritual contract is the profound invitation of the mind of love at this desperate hour.

We invite you to scan your nation, our planet, and the natural world and ask where is there suffering, especially innocent suffering, that you might respond to with love? What dreams do you have of what your society and our world may become? How might you contribute to the birth of a new social contract? How are your daily choices and lifestyle making a difference for love?

Consider your work environment. This may be a home office or a factory, the entertainment business, the medical world, teaching, law enforcement, to name a few. History is witness to the power of the mind of love in action in all of these places and more. Mother Theresa has said that the task is not to do big things but to "do small things with great love." The qualities of generosity, inclusiveness, persistence, spirituality, ethical commitment and wisdom have stood the test of time.

Many of us find ourselves too busy to fully embody and cultivate these transformational aspects of loving action. We encourage you to check in with yourself and your partner and discuss ways that you might act out these qualities in yourselves. The mind of love calls us still, if even in a whisper, regardless of our inner or outer circumstances, to be entangled in the stuff of this precious world. It calls us to be, know, and do our very best to touch and be touched by the great garden of love that is our birthright and the birthright of all beings.

> *The Buddha taught not only the necessity of an inner revolution of the individual for human happiness but also the need for an outer revolution in the life of society."*
>
> —G. P. Malalasekers

Walking at Ground Zero

LARRY WARD

I woke up early and went to Canal Street, which is as far south as you can get in a vehicle on Manhattan. My plan was to make at least 3,000 steps in mindfulness, one for each of the missing people. It was twelve blocks down and six blocks across to Ground Zero. Breathing with each step, I imagined a person in the World Trade Tower, and I offered a silent prayer. I practiced looking into the face of each person that I passed as if it was one of the missing ones. I was aware of some fear, but mostly the sensation of my own deep heartbreak.

As I got closer to Ground Zero, the pungent smell of burning rubber filled my nostrils and a smoke-filled haze irritated my eyes. Ash fell on my eyelashes and caressed my cheek. I continued my slow walking, breathing, and praying with every step for a lost one.

I had my first glimpse of Ground Zero after forty-five minutes of walking. It took me into a deep, deep silence. My mind could not take in what I was witnessing. The site was overflowing with people. Some were just standing and crying. Others were taking pictures or shaking their heads as if in disbelief. The police and military were keeping order in a calm and quiet manner. There was an eerie kind of silence for downtown Manhattan.

The grief at Ground Zero was so thick with substance that it felt like it had erected its own monument to tragedy. My mind could not hold what I was witnessing, so I continued my mindful steps as if circumambulating the entire area. I would walk and then stop to see the site from this angle, and from that angle, and yet another angle.

Two hours into my walking mediation, I began to notice the dust and ash. All the buildings within six or seven blocks of the site were covered with dusty ash. I realized that this was the dust of a policeman, the dust of a fireman, the dust of a maid, secretary, janitor, or stockbroker. Perhaps it was a delivery person who just showed up on their bicycle to deliver a package like they did every other day when they went to work.

The dust of the September 11th tragedy was in me now as I was in it, in every cell of my body, in every mindful step, every fiber of my heart and the mystery of my every breath. I returned home from New York clearer than ever before. This is the exact moment for Maitreya Buddha. Now is the time for, as Thay would say, "Mr. or Ms. Love." Actually, if you look closely and you look deeply into life, you will see him and you will see her already here. Now is the time to deepen our practice of love.

RADIANT LOVING KINDNESS

In loving kindness practice, the quality of compassion is gener-
ated and cultivated in our mind. We begin by extending loving kindness to ourselves. After we've practiced this for some
time, we can begin to extend loving kindness to others. You may
feel that the emotion of deep friendliness should arise spontaneously; that you shouldn't have to work at it. The Buddha
emphasized that although deep friendliness is a heavenly state,
a divine condition of the mind and the heart, it comes *from* us
and not *to* us. Our practice brings it into existence.

> **PRACTICE:** *Radiant Loving Kindness
> in the Ten Directions*

In this practice exercise, often referred to as "Immeasurable
Radiation of Kindness," your feelings of goodness and well-
being are tapped into as a source of kindness that radiates out
from your chest in the region of the heart. It can be helpful to
imagine yourself as a radiant ball of light with takes energy
from all directions and transforms this energy into light. Uncol-
ored light is best suited for radiating metta, the energy of loving
kindness.

1. Settle into your quiet space and enjoy mindful breathing. Sit beautifully, comfortably, solidly. Recall experiences and memories of goodness and loving kindness.
2. Extend loving kindness to yourself: "May I be free
   from danger. May I have mental happiness. May I

have physical happiness. May I have ease of well-being." Let yourself be saturated in the rain of loving kindness.

3. Now imagine all the beings existing in the direction in front of you—beginning from your room, through your neighborhood, and stretching to infinity. Open up your inner space to the direction in front of you. Mentally bend forward without changing your posture, as though you would like to move toward the beings in front of you in order to offer something beneficial and universally good. Reinforce this mental gesture with the loving kindness blessing: "May all beings in front of me be free from danger. May all beings in front of me have mental happiness. May all beings in front of me have physical happiness. May all beings in front of me have ease of well-being." Imagine the energy of loving kindness radiating in front of you through space in time.

4. Imagine all beings existing behind you. Open up your inner space in this direction. Mentally lean toward the rear, as if moving in the direction of all beings behind you. Extend the loving kindness prayer, "May all beings behind me be free from danger. May all beings behind me have mental happiness. May all beings behind me have physical happiness. May all beings behind me have ease of well-being." Imagine extending this radiant energy, this incandescent light behind you and

throughout the room, building, neighborhood, country, and cosmos.

5. Imagine all beings existing to your right. Open up your inner space toward the right. Mentally bend to the right as though you would like to move toward the right. Offer the loving kindness prayer.

6. Imagine all beings below you, under the floor, in the earth, Mother Earth herself, as she lives and breathes, through water, steam, lava, fire, rock, and earth. Extend the radiant light of loving kindness below you and offer the loving kindness prayer.

7. Imagine all beings in the direction above, the sky, clouds, birds, insects, stars, and galaxies, beings in the upper world, gods, devas, angels, all beings above you. Open yourself toward the space above you and radiate the energy of loving kindness above. Offer the loving kindness prayer. Imagine radiant beams of loving kindness reaching over head.

8. Open yourself in all the directions, radiating loving kindness from a ball of light. Offer the loving kindness prayer. Expand the light outward from your heart in all directions, radiating love throughout the room, neighborhood, community, country, planet, cosmos.

9. Focus the radiant light to your own body, to your heart space, which can be visualized as a ball of light, and offer the loving kindness prayer. Imagine every cell of your body pulsing with the energy of light and love.

10. Close the meditation time. Extend the merit of the practice for the good of all beings. Make sure you are good and grounded before driving—take a walk, make some notes. What did you learn about love today? What do you know about love in this moment?

PRACTICE: *Metta Meditation*

Sit quietly. Repeat these words. Breathe. Take breaths when you need to.

+ May I/you/we be peaceful, happy, and light in body and spirit.
+ May I/you/we be safe and free from injury.
+ May I/you/we be free from anger, affliction, fear, and anxiety.
+ May I/you/we learn to look at myself with the eyes of understanding and love.
+ May I/you/we be able to recognize and touch the seeds of joy and happiness in myself.
+ May I/you/we learn to identify and see the sources of anger, craving, and delusion in myself.
+ May I/you/we know how to nourish the seeds of joy in myself every day.
+ May I/you/we be able to live fresh, solid, and free.
+ May I/you/we be free from attachment and aversion but not be indifferent.

— from *Chanting from the Heart,* Thich Nhat Hanh

CHAPTER TWELVE

Being Love's Gardener

True love is a very concrete practice. It fundamentally affects how we live our daily lives and make our daily decisions. Bodhisattvas, enlightened beings who commit themselves to loving all beings, feed themselves the spiritual, emotional, and material food that nourishes and cultivates their mind of love. By feeding ourselves with things that nourish our mind of love, we can become bodhisattvas.

In the summer of 2003, Thich Nhat Hanh said something that we continue to reflect on. He said, "Be a real human being." What does it mean to be a real human being? A real human being recognizes that he or she is a guest on this planet. The earth supports and nourishes us; the streams and trees accept us. We all have the capacity to be greedy, to want too much, to give too little to ourselves as well as to others. But these things are just shadows passing across the ground of the real human being. It is our practice of watering the seeds in ourselves and others that gives us a chance to be a real human being. Our practice is to create an environment that gives us a chance to blossom and be ourselves. With our partner, we have a wonderful opportunity to practice cultivating our best self.

A real human being recognizes that he or she is a renter, a guest on earth. The earth is here supporting us and holding us. The creek is here and the trees are here accepting and supporting us. We are the guests. In the morning when the sunlight strikes the sky for the first time, you can see dust in the beams of sunlight. A real human being is the sunlight, not the dust. Our practice is to water those seeds in us that give us a deep chance to be a real human being and to create an environment where all beings can blossom

In the Buddhist tradition, real human beings have been called "worthy ones" and "noble ones." If you want to do something with your life, be a real human being. If you want to do something for your children or your grandchildren, be a real human being. If you want to do something for your society or the planet, be a real human being. Everything you need is already inside of you, in every cell of your body. Develop it, cultivate it, and apply it. One of the Buddha's fundamental insights is: With practice, every one of us can live life deeply and fully, surrounded by love. This was our undertaking in *Love's Garden*.

We thank you for your commitment to love beautifully.

We are inspired by your practice of growing your hearts as wide as the world.

We want to encourage your aspiration to live beautifully and love shamelessly.

We are grateful for your love that grows in ever-widening circles.

Thank you for your practice and presence of true love in the world.

Put this up somewhere in your life where you can see it every-day. "He or she who wants to attain peace should practice being upright, humble, and capable of using loving speech. He or she will know how to live simply and happily, with senses calmed, without being covetous and carried away by the emotions of the majority. Let him or her not do anything that will be disap-proved of by the wise ones.

"(And this is what he or she contemplates):

"May everyone be happy and safe, and may all hearts be filled with joy.

"May all beings live in security and in peace—beings who are frail or strong, tall or short, big or small, invisible or visible, near or faraway, already born, or yet to be born. May all of them dwell in perfect tranquility.

"Let no one do harm to anyone. Let no one put the life of anyone in danger. Let no one, out of anger or ill will, wish any-one any harm.

"Just as a mother loves and protects her only child at the risk of her own life, cultivate boundless love to offer to all living beings in the entire cosmos. Let our boundless love pervade the whole universe, above, below, and across. Our love will know no obstacles. Our heart will be absolutely free from hatred and enmity. Whether standing or walking, sitting or lying, as long as we are awake, we should maintain this mindfulness of love in our own heart. This is the noblest way of living.

"Free from wrong views, greed, and sensual desires, living in beauty and realizing Perfect Understanding, those who practice boundless love will certainly transcend birth and death."

—Metta Sutta, Sutta Nipata 1.8
(as translated by Thich Nhat Hanh
in *Chanting from the Heart*)

In the Changing Room

by Larry Ward

White and red dogwood trees reach toward blue sky
Yellow daffodils shoot up from the earth
Bright forsythia everywhere, swaying in the gentle breeze
The warmth of the sun, the freshness of spring, is in me, too.
Opening, growing, smiling to life.

There is not much time left.
The earth continues to turn
I am certain now of what I must do
I am out of rhythm with the one who knows
I steal moments to come home to myself
In the still of the night
I sing the songs of silence.
At the dawn of the day
I find my breath in the gentle mist
Robins sing outside my window
I hear the sound of ducks winging their way
over the pond.
It takes time to offer the best to myself.
I have not had it and it makes me sad.

A beam of moonlight changed everything.
A ride on the Perfume River brought me all the way home.
Floating candles on dark water

Heart wishes drift across rivers of time.
"Please stay in the Pagoda" says the Abbot.
If only I could.

I am here now,
waking up in the changing room
of my soul's department store.
I am becoming what my young self once knew.
Gazing at stars from the attic window.
following a yellow and green caterpillar
on the sidewalks of Cleveland to new worlds.

Books
Poems
Songs
Preaching love
and being in love
is all I ever wanted.

Acknowledgments

We extend our gratitude to our root teacher, Thich Nhat Hanh. Thank you for being with us every step of the way. Our love for you, dear Thay, knows no boundary.

We are grateful to Deer Park, Plum Village, Maple Forest and Blue Cliff Monasteries, and Great Tree Zen Women's Temple for your deep practice and gift of loving friendship. Thanks to The Bright Path, Clear View, Beginner's Mind, Wabi Sabi, Mountain Mindfulness, Cloud Cottage, and Blue Heron Sanghas, Windsong Dojo, Pendle Hill, Abbey North, the Univeristy of Oklahoma City Department of Religion, and Southern Dharma Retreat Center. Thank you Travis, Rachel Neumann, and Parallax Press for your belief in us and your editorial wisdom and support for the publication of *Love's Garden*. Barbara Casey, Baba, dear friend, thank you for walking through the writing and editing. Thank you for helping us collect the writings. Robert Sorrell, thank you for photographs and musical inspiration. Miriam and Harley Goldberg, we thank you for your faith, love, and sharing the gift of freedom that is possible in a long-term marriage. Tina Spencer, your gift helped this book happen. Nick and Louise Rich, we are grateful for your love and friendship. Azimat Lane Schultz, perfect timing for the gift of editing and friendship, thank you. Matthew Bortolin and Heather, thank you for writing and friendship. Karen Hilsberg and Alexa Singer-Telles, thank you for sharing your writing, poetry, and your support for us as teachers. Gratia Meyer, thank you for offering your vow as a living testimony to great love. David McCleskey and Patricia Webb, we are grateful for your support of us as friends and teachers. Sara and Steve Becker, thank you for your writing and support. Kim Hsieh and Grant, your love and your writing inspire us. Thanks to Ariel Blair for all your editorial support of our writing and for being our sister. Thanks to our friends and writers Carolyn Marsden, Jayna Gieber, Lisa Pettit, Susan Glogovac, Harriet Wrye-Kimball, Norma Bradley, Victoria Emerson, Susana Ayala-Gabriel, and Emily Whittle. To our teachers, Angeles Arrien, Jean Houston, Peggy Rubin, Gay Luce, Joe Matthews, Marion Woodman, Pema Chodron and Chungliang Huang. For friendship and more: Judie McReynolds and George, Suzanne Lewis, Nate Terry, Barbara Knudson, Andre Watts, Joan Brand, Gael Belden, Chris Dawkins, Brad and Brenda Wiscons, Karen Vizzina, Hollye Hurst, Jeanette Reid, Teijo, Kichung, Anne Clement, Elizbeth Mueller, Penny and Jim, John Roberts, Chris Binion, Yogananda, Gay Whitesides, Nancy Budge, Scott and M'Tae, Salvatore Caruso, Dianne and Dharce Greenwald, Peter and Ellen, John and Thea Patterson, Rob, Jen, and Chris Work, Peter and Lisa Peterson, John and Susan Turner, Mike and Kay Sherlock, Verna and Equal Smith, Lien Ho, Dr. John Harrison and Allison Brietl-Reid, you are all in our hearts and in this book.

Bibliography

The Four Fold Way, Angeles Arrien
(New York, NY: HarperOne, 1993).

The Second Half of Life, Angeles Arrien
(Boulder, CO: Sounds True, 2007).

Start Where You Are, Pema Chodron
(Boston, MA: Shambhala, 2001).

The Wisdom of No Escape, Pema Chodron
(Boston, MA: Shambhala, 2001).

Watch Me Fly, Myrlie Evers-Williams
(New York, NY: Little Brown, 1999).

Compassion, Christina Feldman
(Berkeley, CA: Rodmell Press, 2005).

The Practice of Happiness, Mirko Fryba,
(Boston, MA: Shambhala, 1995).

Call Me By My True Names, Thich Nhat Hanh
(Berkeley, CA: Parallax Press, 1999).

Chanting from the Heart, Thich Nhat Hanh
(Berkeley, CA: Parallax Press, 2007).

For a Future to Be Possible, Thich Nhat Hanh
(Berkeley, CA: Parallax Press, 1998).

Fragrant Palm Leaves, Thich Nhat Hanh
(Berkeley, CA: Parallax Press, 1998).

Teachings on Love, Thich Nhat Hanh
(Berkeley, CA: Parallax Press, 1998, 2007).

The Heart of the Buddha's Teachings, Thich Nhat Hanh
(Berkeley, CA: Parallax Press, 1998;
New York, NY: Broadway Books, 1999).

Into the Garden: A Wedding Anthology, Robert Hass
and Stephen Mitchell (New York, NY: Harper, 1994).

The Story of My Life, Helen Keller
(New York, NY: Pocket Books, 1996).

Ruling Your World, Sakyong Mipham
(New York, NY: Broadway Books, 2005).

Turning the Mind into an Ally, Sakyong Mipham
(New York, NY: Riverhead Books, 2003).

The Words of My Perfect Teacher, Patrul Rinpoche
(Boston, MA: Shambhala, 1998).

Making Friends with Time, Peggy Rowe Ward
and Tracy Sarriugarte (Newton, MA: PBJ Press, 1999).

A Grateful Heart, edited by M. J. Ryan
(New York, NY: Fine Communications, 1997).

A Heart as Wide as the World, Sharon Salzberg
(Boston, MA: Shambhala, 1999).

Loving Kindness, Sharon Salzberg
(Boston, MA: Shambhala, 1995).

Bring Me the Rhinoceros, John Tarrant
(New York, NY: Harmony, 2004).

Parallax Press, a nonprofit organization, publishes books on engaged Buddhism and the practice of mindfulness by Thich Nhat Hanh and other authors. All of Thich Nhat Hanh's work is available at our online store and in our free catalog. For a copy of the catalog, please contact:

Parallax Press
P.O. Box 7355
Berkeley, CA 94707
Tel: (510) 525-0101
www.parallax.org

Monastics and laypeople practice the art of mindful living in the tradition of Thich Nhat Hanh at retreat communities in France and the United States. To reach any of these communities, or for information about individuals and families joining for a practice period, please contact:

Plum Village
13 Martineau
33580 Dieulivol, France
info@plumvillage.org

Blue Cliff Monastery
3 Mindfulness Road
Pine Bush, NY 12566
www.bluecliffmonastery.org

Deer Park Monastery
2499 Melru Lane
Escondido, CA 92026
deerpark@plumvillage.org

The *Mindfulness Bell*, a Journal of the Art of Mindful Living in the Tradition of Thich Nhat Hanh, is published three times a year by Plum Village. To subscribe or to see the worldwide directory of Sanghas, visit www.mindfulnessbell.org.